Effective Ruby

The Effective Software Development Series

Scott Meyers, Consulting Editor

Addison-Wesley

Visit **informit.com/esds** for a complete list of available publications.

The **Effective Software Development Series** provides expert advice on all aspects of modern software development. Titles in the series are well written, technically sound, and of lasting value. Each describes the critical things experts always do — or always avoid — to produce outstanding software.

Scott Meyers, author of the best-selling books *Effective C++* (now in its third edition), *More Effective C++*, and *Effective STL* (all available in both print and electronic versions), conceived of the series and acts as its consulting editor. Authors in the series work with Meyers to create essential reading in a format that is familiar and accessible for software developers of every stripe.

Make sure to connect with us!
informit.com/socialconnect

informIT.com
the trusted technology learning source | **Addison-Wesley** | **Safari**
Books Online

Effective Ruby

48 Specific Ways to Write Better Ruby

Peter J. Jones

✦ Addison-Wesley

Upper Saddle River, NJ • Boston • Indianapolis • San Francisco
New York • Toronto • Montreal • London • Munich • Paris • Madrid
Capetown • Sydney • Tokyo • Singapore • Mexico City

Many of the designations used by manufacturers and sellers to distinguish their products are claimed as trademarks. Where those designations appear in this book, and the publisher was aware of a trademark claim, the designations have been printed with initial capital letters or in all capitals.

The author and publisher have taken care in the preparation of this book, but make no expressed or implied warranty of any kind and assume no responsibility for errors or omissions. No liability is assumed for incidental or consequential damages in connection with or arising out of the use of the information or programs contained herein.

For information about buying this title in bulk quantities, or for special sales opportunities (which may include electronic versions; custom cover designs; and content particular to your business, training goals, marketing focus, or branding interests), please contact our corporate sales department at corpsales@pearsoned.com or (800) 382-3419.

For government sales inquiries, please contact governmentsales@pearsoned.com.

For questions about sales outside the United States, please contact international@pearsoned.com.

Visit us on the Web: informit.com/aw

Library of Congress Cataloging-in-Publication Data
Jones, Peter J., author.
  Effective Ruby : 48 specific ways to write better Ruby / Peter J. Jones.
    Pages   cm
  Includes index.
  ISBN 978-0-13-384697-3 (pbk. : alk. paper)
  1. Ruby (Computer program language) 2. Object-oriented programming
(Computer science) I. Title.
  QA76.73.R83J66 2015
  005.13'3—dc23
                                        2014026572

ISBN-13: 978-0-13-384697-3
ISBN-10: 0-13-384697-0
Text printed in the United States on recycled paper at RR Donnelley, Crawfordsville, Indiana.
First printing, September 2014

Editor-in-Chief
Mark L. Taub

Senior Acquisitions Editor
Trina MacDonald

Development Editor
Songlin Qiu

Managing Editor
John Fuller

Full-Service Production Manager
Julie B. Nahil

Copy Editor
Christina Edwards

Indexer
Jack Lewis

Proofreader
Andrea Fox

Technical Reviewers
Bruce Williams
Bobby Wilson

Editorial Assistant
Olivia Basegio

Cover Designer
Chuti Prasertsith

Compositor
LaurelTech

For Shanna, the reason my life has balance and purpose.

Contents

Foreword

When I was asked to do a technical review and write the foreword for a book on Ruby, I was skeptical. Several Ruby books already exist that run the gamut from beginner to advanced Ruby VM internals. I thought, "What could *another* Ruby book offer?" But I agreed to look over the text, and to my surprise a great and novel book about Ruby was laid out before my eyes. This book is quite unlike any other Ruby book, and in a couple hundred pages, I imagine anyone who reads this—novice or expert—will emerge a better Ruby programmer.

Ruby as a language has matured a lot in the past decade, when I got started with it. Early on, there was the hype phase, when Ruby was touted as the end-all and be-all of languages. Then emerged the proliferation of libraries, when it felt like libraries were being abandoned and re-created daily, and none could be trusted to remain up to date. Then other "new hotness" languages started emerging, and Ruby went through a phase of being seen as the language of yesteryear. But now, finally, Ruby is seen as a practical, effective language for solving many problems, although it understandably won't solve all of them. (You're not going to be writing the next big operating system in Ruby.)

Instead of being a book that covers basic syntax or advanced practices, this book masterfully walks the line of introducing real-world best practices for writing Ruby applications that won't crash, will be maintainable, and will be fast. It is a book that every Ruby programmer should read. Beginners should learn best practices to better understand the language, and experienced developers should double-check their own practices and maybe learn a couple of new ones as well.

The book is written in my favorite way: lots of examples, and the examples don't just explain "What?" and "How?", but also "Why?" Although these are best practices curated from the Ruby community over years of maturation, it is important to always remain skeptical, ask questions, and perhaps find new best practices that improve on the old.

With that, I wish you a fun journey through this book, and fully expect you to grow as a Ruby programmer in just a couple hundred pages.

—*Mitchell Hashimoto, founder and CEO of HashiCorp, creator of Vagrant*

Preface

Learning a new programming language usually happens in two phases. During the first phase you spend time learning the syntax and structure of the language. This phase is often short when you have previous experience learning new programming languages. In the case of Ruby, the syntax is very familiar to those who have experience with other object-oriented languages. The structure of the language—how you build programs out of the syntax—should also be very familiar to experienced programmers.

The second phase, on the other hand, can take a bit more work. This is when you dig deeper into the language and learn its idioms. Most languages have a unique way of solving common problems, and Ruby is no different. For example, Ruby uses blocks along with the iterator pattern instead of explicit looping. Learning how to solve problems "the Ruby way" while avoiding any sharp edges is what this phase is all about.

And that's what this book is all about, too. But it's not an introductory book. I assume you've already completed the first phase of learning Ruby—that is, learning its syntax and structure. My goal with this book is to take you deeper into Ruby. I want to show you how to get the most out of the language and how to write effective code that is more reliable and easier to maintain. Along the way we'll also explore how parts of the Ruby interpreter work internally, knowledge that will allow you to write more efficient programs.

Ruby Implementations and Versions

As you know, Ruby has a very active community of contributors. They work on all sorts of projects, including different implementations of the Ruby interpreter. Besides the official Ruby implementation (colloquially known as MRI), there are several others to choose from. Need to deploy your Ruby application to production servers that are already configured for running Java applications? No problem, that's what JRuby is for. How about the opposite end of the spectrum, Ruby applications targeting smartphones and tablets? There's a Ruby implementation for that, too.

Having several Ruby implementations to choose from is a good sign that Ruby is alive and well. Obviously, each of them has a unique, internal implementation. But from the perspective of a programmer writing Ruby code, the various interpreters behave closely enough to MRI that you won't have to worry much.

The vast majority of this book applies equally to all of the various Ruby implementations. The only exceptions are the items that describe Ruby internal details such as how the garbage collector works. In those cases, I will narrow my focus to the official Ruby implementation, MRI. You'll know when we're talking about MRI specifically when I mention specific Ruby versions in the text.

Speaking of specific versions, all of the code in this book has been tested with Ruby 1.9.3 and later. At the time of writing, Ruby 2.1 was the most recent version, with 2.2 just around the corner. When I don't mention a specific version of Ruby in the text, the example code will work on all supported versions.

A Note about Style

Ruby programmers have, for the most part, converged on a single way of formatting their Ruby code. There are even a handful of Ruby-Gems that can inspect your code and scold you when it isn't format-ted according to a set of predetermined styling rules. I bring this up because the style I've chosen for the example code in this book devi-ates slightly from what might be considered normal.

When I call a method and supply arguments to it, I use parenthe-ses around the arguments, without any space between the opening parenthesis and the name of the method. Out in the wild, it's com-mon to see method calls *without* parentheses, probably because Ruby doesn't require them. But as we'll see in Chapter 1, omitting paren-theses in some situations can cause ambiguities in your code, which in turn forces Ruby to guess what you mean. Because of these ambi-guities, I think it's a bad habit to omit parentheses and one the com-munity needs to wean itself from.

The other reason I use parentheses is to clearly show when an iden-tifier is a method call versus a keyword. You might be surprised to learn that things you thought were keywords are actually method calls (e.g., `require`). Using parentheses helps illustrate this.

While we're on the topic of style, I should mention that throughout this book, when I mention methods, I use RI notation. If you're not familiar with RI notation it's easy to learn and can be very helpful. Its primary purpose is to differentiate between class and instance methods. When referring to class methods I'll write the name of the class and the method separated by two colons ("::"). For example, File::open is the open class method from the File class. Likewise, instance methods are written with a number sign ("#") between the class name and the name of the instance method (e.g., Array#each). The same is true of module methods (e.g., GC::stat) and module instance methods (e.g., Enumerable#grep). Item 40 goes into more detail about RI notation and how to use it to look up method documentation. But this little primer is enough to get you started.

Where to Get the Source Code

Throughout the book we'll examine many listings of example source code. To make it easier to digest, code will often be broken up into small chunks that we'll work though one at a time. There are even times when unimportant details are omitted. Sometimes it's nice to see all the code at once, to get the bigger picture, so to speak. All of the code shown can be found at the website for the book at http://effectiveruby.com.

Acknowledgments

Writing something that people are willing to spend their time reading, and something worthy of spending their money on, isn't a solo endeavor. As a matter of fact, beyond the close group of people who were directly involved in this book, many others unknowingly contributed in one way or another. For example, my friend Michael Garriss had no idea what the consequences of his actions would be when he sweet-talked me into learning Ruby. He certainly didn't expect for me to drag him from company to company, introducing Ruby at each step of the way. Nevertheless, that's what happened.

It might be a bit unorthodox (and vague) but I want to thank everyone who's ever contributed their time and creativity to the open-source community. Every single tool I used while writing this book, even those I created specifically for it, are open-source projects. There's no way I could have written this book without being able to review the source code to the Ruby interpreter and the handful of gems that are discussed. I spent many hours curled up with code, dissecting, experimenting, and sometimes crying. The fact that I was able to do that is wonderful all by itself.

Of course, without the generosity of those who volunteered to work with me, this book wouldn't be worthy of your attention. Several people gave up their free time to review early drafts of the chapters and provided me with immensely useful feedback. Isaac Foraker, Timothy Clayton, and my wife, Shanna Jones, spent many hours reading text and experimenting with code. Thank you so much for your time.

Probably not realizing what they were getting themselves into, Bruce Williams and Bobby Wilson agreed to be technical reviewers. They both helped me improve the examples in the book and the explanations that go along with them. They also encouraged me when the anxiety of having someone else poking around my work was a bit overwhelming.

Everyone at Pearson made things as easy for me as they could. Trina MacDonald, Olivia Basegio, and Songlin Qiu were extremely patient with me and shaped this book into what it is now. I've grown so much during this project and a large part of that is due to them.

Scott Meyers is a hero of mine and being able to work with him is like having a dream come true. In the late 1990s I came across Scott's book, *Effective C++*, and it changed the way I approached programming. It also inspired me to teach others the things I have learned. Sending my work to Scott for review was terrifying, but Scott was nothing less than encouraging and extremely helpful. Thank you, Scott.

My wife, Shanna Jones, was a huge source of encouragement and understanding. Knowing that it would take me away from her, she pushed me to write this book anyway. Shanna, you've taught me more than you understand. Thank you for always supporting me.

About the Author

Peter J. Jones has been working professionally with Ruby since 2005. He began programming before he learned how to use a keyboard properly after stumbling upon a Commodore 64, a few code listings, and some cassette tapes. Peter is a freelance software engineer and a senior instructor for programming related workshops taught by Devalot.com.

Accustoming Yourself to Ruby

With each programming language you learn, it's important to dig in and discover its idiosyncrasies. Ruby is no different. While it borrows heavily from the languages that preceded it, Ruby certainly has its own way of doing things. And sometimes those ways will surprise you.

We begin our journey through Ruby's many features by examining its unique take on common programming ideas. That is, those that impact every part of your program. With these items mastered, you'll be prepared to tackle the chapters that follow.

Item 1: Understand What Ruby Considers to Be True

Every programming language seems to have its own way of dealing with Boolean values. Some languages only have a single representation of true or false. Others have a confusing blend of types that are sometimes true and sometimes false. Failure to understand which values are true and which are false can lead to bugs in conditional expressions. For example, how many languages do you know where the number zero is false? What about those where zero is true?

Ruby has its own way of doing things, Boolean values included. Thankfully, the rule for figuring out if a value is true or false is pretty simple. It's different than other languages, which is the whole reason this item exists, so make sure you understand what follows. In Ruby, every value is true *except* false and nil.

It's worth taking a moment and thinking about what this means. While it's a simple rule, it has some strange consequences when compared with other mainstream languages. In a lot of programming languages the number zero is false, with all other numbers being true. Using the rule just given for Ruby, zero is *true*. That's probably one of the biggest gotchas for programmers coming to Ruby from other languages.

Another trick that Ruby plays on you if you're coming from another language is the assumption that true and false are keywords. They're not. In fact, they're best described as global variables that don't follow the naming and assignment rules. What I mean by this is that they don't begin with a "$" character, like most global variables, and they can't be used as the left-hand side of an assignment. But in all other regards they're global variables. See for yourself:

```
irb> true.class
---> TrueClass

irb> false.class
---> FalseClass
```

As you can see, true and false act like global objects, and like any object, you can call methods on them. (Ruby also defines TRUE and FALSE constants that reference these true and false objects.) They also come from two different classes: TrueClass and FalseClass. Neither of these classes allows you to create new objects from them; true and false are all we get. Knowing the rule Ruby uses for conditional expressions, you can see that the true object only exists for convenience. Since false and nil are the only false values, the true object is superfluous for representing a true value. Any non-false, non-nil object can do that for you.

Having two values to represent false and all others to represent true can sometimes get in your way. One common example is when you need to differentiate between false and nil. This comes up all the time in objects that represent configuration information. In those objects, a false value means that something should be disabled, while a nil value means an option wasn't explicitly specified and the default value should be used instead. The easiest way to tell them apart is by using the nil? method, which is described further in Item 2. Another way is by using the "==" operator with false used as the left operand:

```
if false == x.
  ...
end
```

With some languages there's a stylistic rule that says you should always use immutable constants as the left-hand side of an equality operator. That's not why I'm recommending false as the left operand to the "==" operator. In this case, it's important for a functional reason. Placing false on the left-hand side means that Ruby parses the expression as a call to the FalseClass#== method (which comes from the Object class). We can rest safely knowing this method only returns true if the right operand is also the false object. On the other hand, using false as the *right* operand may not work as expected since other classes can override the Object#== method and loosen the comparison:

```
irb> class Bad
        def == (other)
           true
        end
     end

irb> false == Bad.new
---> false
irb> Bad.new == false
---> true
```

Of course, something like this would be pretty silly. But in my experience, that means it's more likely to happen. (By the way, we'll cover the "==" operator more in Item 12.)

Things to Remember

◆ Every value is true *except* false and nil.

◆ Unlike in a lot of languages, the number zero is true in Ruby.

◆ If you need to differentiate between false and nil, either use the nil? method or use the "==" operator with false as the left operand.

Item 2: Treat All Objects as If They Could Be nil

Every object in a running Ruby program comes from a class that, in one way or another, inherits from the BasicObject class. Imagining how all these objects relate to one another should conjure up the familiar tree diagram with BasicObject at the root. What this means in practice is that an object of one class can be substituted for an object of another (thanks to polymorphism). That's why we can pass an object that *behaves* like an array—but is not actually an array—to a method that expects an Array object. Ruby programmers like to call this "duck typing." Instead of requiring that an object be an instance of a specific class, duck typing shifts the focus to what the object can do; in other words, interface over type. In Ruby terms, duck typing means you should prefer using the respond_to? method over the is_a? method.

But in reality, it's rare to see a method inspect its arguments using respond_to? to make sure it supports the correct interface. Instead, we tend to just invoke methods on an object and if the object doesn't respond to a particular method, we leave it up to Ruby to raise a

NoMethodError exception at run time. On the surface, it seems like this could be a real problem for Ruby programmers. Well, just between you and me, it is. It's one of the core reasons testing is so very important. There's nothing stopping you from accidentally passing a Time object to a method expecting a Date object. These are the kinds of mistakes we have to tease out with good tests. And thanks to testing, these types of problems can be avoided. But one of these polymorphic substitutions plagues even well-tested applications:

```
undefined method 'fubar' for nil:NilClass (NoMethodError)
```

This is what happens when you call a method on an object and it turns out to be that pesky nil object...the one and only object from the NilClass class. Errors like this tend to slip through testing only to show up in production when a user does something out of the ordinary. Another situation where this can occur is when a method returns nil and then that return value gets passed directly into another method as an argument. There's a surprisingly large number of ways nil can unexpectedly get introduced into your running program. The best defense is to assume that any object might actually be the nil object. This includes arguments passed to methods and return values from them.

One of the easiest ways to avoid invoking methods on the nil object is by using the nil? method. It returns true if the receiver is nil and false otherwise. Of course, nil objects are always false in a Boolean context, so the if and unless expressions work as expected. All of the following lines are equivalent to one another:

```
person.save if person
person.save if !person.nil?
person.save unless person.nil?
```

It's often easier to explicitly convert a variable into the expected type rather than worry about nil all the time. This is especially true when a method should produce a result even if some of its inputs are nil. The Object class defines several conversion methods that can come in handy in this case. For example, the to_s method converts the receiver into a string:

```
irb> 13.to_s
---> "13"

irb> nil.to_s
---> ""
```

As you can see, NilClass#to_s returns an empty string. What makes to_s really nice is that String#to_s simply returns self without performing any conversion or copying. If a variable is already a string then using to_s will have minimal overhead. But if nil somehow winds up where a string is expected, to_s can save the day. As an example, suppose a method expects one of its arguments to be a string. Using to_s, you can hedge against that argument being nil:

```ruby
def fix_title (title)
  title.to_s.capitalize
end
```

The fun doesn't stop there. As you'd expect, there's a matching conversion method for almost all of the built-in classes. Here are some of the more useful ones as they apply to nil:

```
irb> nil.to_a
---> []

irb> nil.to_i
---> 0

irb> nil.to_f
---> 0.0
```

When multiple values are being considered at the same time, you can make use of a neat trick from the Array class. The Array#compact method returns a copy of the receiver with all nil elements removed. It's common to use it for constructing a string out of a set of variables that might be nil. For example, if a person's name is made up of first, middle, and last components—any of which might be nil—you can construct a complete full name with the following code:

```ruby
name = [first, middle, last].compact.join(" ")
```

The nil object has a tendency to sneak into your running programs when you least expect it. Whether it's from user input, an unconstrained database, or methods that return nil to signal failure, always assume that every variable could be nil.

Things to Remember

+ Due to the way Ruby's type system works, any object can be nil.

+ The nil? method returns true if its receiver is nil and false otherwise.

+ When appropriate, use conversion methods such as to_s and to_i to coerce nil objects into the expected type.

+ The Array#compact method returns a copy of the receiver with all nil elements removed.

Item 3: Avoid Ruby's Cryptic Perlisms

If you've ever used the Perl programming language then you undoubt-
edly recognize its influence on Ruby. The majority of Ruby's perlisms
have been adopted in such a way that they blend perfectly with the
rest of the ecosystem. But others either stick out like an unnecessary
semicolon or are so obscure that they leave you scratching your head
trying to figure out how a particular piece of code works.

Over the years, as Ruby matured, alternatives to some of the more
cryptic perlisms were added. As more time went on, some of these
holdovers from Perl were deprecated or even completely removed from
Ruby. Yet, a few still remain, and you're likely to come across them
in the wild. This item can be used as a guide to deciphering those
perlisms while acting as a warning to avoid introducing them into
your own code.

The corner of Ruby where you're most likely to encounter features borrowed from Perl is a set of cryptic global variables. In fact, Ruby has
some pretty liberal naming rules when it comes to global variables.
Unlike with local variables, instance variables, or even constants,
you're allowed to use all sorts of characters as variable names. Recall-
ing that global variables begin with a "$" character, consider this:

```
def extract_error (message)
  if message =~ /^ERROR:\s+(.+)$/
    $1
  else
    "no error"
  end
end
```

There are two perlisms packed into this code example. The first is the
use of the "=~" operator from the String class. It returns the position
within the string where the right operand (usually a regular expression) matches, or nil if no match can be found. When the regular
expression matches, several global variables will be set so you can
extract information from the string. In this example, I'm extracting
the contents of the first capture group using the $1 global variable.
And this is where things get a bit weird. That variable might look and
smell like a global variable, but it surely doesn't act like one.

The variables created by the "=~" operator are called *special* global variables. That's because they're scoped *locally* to the current thread and
method. Essentially, they're local values with global names. Outside of
the extract_error method from the previous example, the $1 "global"
variable is nil, even after using the "=~" operator. In the example,

returning the value of the $1 variable is just like returning the value of a local variable. The whole situation can be confusing. The good news is that it's completely unnecessary. Consider this alternative:

```
def extract_error (message)
  if m = message.match(/^ERROR:\s+(.+)$/)
    m[1]
  else
    "no error"
  end
end
```

Using String#match is much more idiomatic and doesn't use any of the special global variables set by the "=~" operator. That's because the match method returns a MatchData object (when the regular expression matches) and it contains all of the same information that was previously available in those special global variables. In this version of the extract_error method, you can see that using the index operator with a value of 1 gives you the same string that $1 would have given you in the previous example. The bonus feature is that the MatchData object is a plain old local variable and you get to choose the name of it. (It's fairly common to make an assignment inside the conditional part of an if expression like this. That said, it's all too easy to use "=" when you really meant "==". Watch out for these kinds of mistakes.)

Besides those set by the "=~" operator, there are other global variables borrowed from Perl. The one you're most likely to see is $:, which is an array of strings representing the directories where Ruby will search for libraries that are loaded with the require method. Instead of using the $: global variable, you should use its more descriptive alias: $LOAD_PATH. As a matter of fact, there are more descriptive versions for all of the other cryptic global variables such as $; and $/. But there's a catch. Unlike with $LOAD_PATH, you have to load a library to access the other global variables' aliases:

```
require('English')
```

Once the English library is loaded, you can replace all those strange global variables by their longer, more descriptive aliases. For a full list of these aliases, take a look at the documentation for the English module.

There's one last perlism you should be aware of. Not surprisingly, it also has something to do with a global variable. Consider this:

```
while readline
  print if ~ /^ERROR:/
end
```

If you think this code is a bit obfuscated, then congratulations, you're in good company. You might be wondering what the print method is actually printing and what that regular expression is matching against. It just so happens that all of the methods in this example are working with a global variable—the $_ variable to be more precise.

So, what's going on here? It all starts with the readline method. More specifically, it's the Kernel#readline method. (In Item 6, we'll dig more into how Ruby determines that, in this context, readline comes from the Kernel module.) This version of readline is a little different from its counterpart in the IO class. You can probably gather that it reads a line from standard input and returns it. The subtle part is that it also stores that line of input in the $_ variable. (Kernel#gets does the same thing but doesn't raise an exception when the end-of-file marker is reached.) In a similar fashion, if Kernel#print is called without any arguments, it will print the contents of the $_ variable to standard output.

You can probably guess what that unary "~" operator and the regular expression are doing. The Regexp#~ operator tries to match the contents of the $_ variable against the regular expression to its right. If there's a match, it returns the position of the match; otherwise, it returns nil. While all these methods might look like they are somehow magically working together, you now know that it's all thanks to the $_ global variable. But why does Ruby even support this?

The only legitimate use for these methods (and the $_ variable) is for writing short, simple scripts on the command line, so-called "one liners." This allows Ruby to compete with tools such as Perl, awk, and sed. When you're writing real code you should avoid methods that implicitly read from, or write to, the $_ global variable. These include other similar Kernel methods I haven't listed here such as chomp, sub, and gsub. The difference with those is that they can no longer be used in recent versions of Ruby without using either the "-n" or the "-p" command-line option to the Ruby interpreter. That is, it's like these methods don't even exist without one of those command-line options. That's a good thing.

Now you can see how some of the more cryptic perlisms can affect the readability, and thus maintainability, of your code. Especially those obscure global variables and the ones that are global in name only. It is best to use the more Ruby-like methods (String#match vs. String#=~) and the longer, more descriptive names for global variables ($LOAD_PATH vs. $:).

Things to Remember

+ Prefer String#match to String#=~. The former returns all the match information in a MatchData object instead of several special global variables.

+ Use the longer, more descriptive global variable aliases as opposed to their short cryptic names (e.g., $LOAD_PATH instead of $:). Most of the longer names are only available after loading the English library.

+ Avoid methods that implicitly read from, or write to, the $_ global variable (e.g., Kernel#print, Regexp#~, etc.).

Item 4: Be Aware That Constants Are Mutable

If you're coming to Ruby from another programming language, there's a good chance that constants don't behave the way you expect them to. But before we dig into that let's review what Ruby considers to be a constant.

When you first learned Ruby you were probably taught that constants are identifiers that are made up of uppercase alphanumeric characters and underscores. Some examples include STDIN, ARGV, and RUBY_VERSION. But that's not the entire story. In reality, a constant is any identifier that begins with an uppercase letter. This means that identifiers like String and Array are also constants. That's right...the names of classes and modules are actually constants in Ruby. With that in mind, let's take a closer look at how constants differ from other variable-like things in Ruby.

As their name suggests, constants are meant to remain unchanged during the lifetime of a program. You might assume, therefore, that Ruby would prevent you from altering the value stored in a constant. Well, that assumption would be wrong. Consider this:

```ruby
module Defaults
  NETWORKS = ["192.168.1", "192.168.2"]
end
def purge_unreachable (networks=Defaults::NETWORKS)
  networks.delete_if do |net|
    !ping(net + ".1")
  end
end
```

If you invoke the purge_unreachable method without an argument, it will accidentally mutate a constant. It will do this without so much as a warning from Ruby. Essentially, constants are more like global variables than unchanging values. If you think about it, since class and module names are constants, and you can change a class at anytime (e.g., add methods), then the objects referenced by constants need to be mutable in Ruby. That's fine for classes and modules, but not so great for the values we actually want to be constant and immutable. Thankfully, there's a solution to this problem—the freeze method:

```ruby
module Defaults
  NETWORKS = ["192.168.1", "192.168.2"].freeze
end
```

With this change in place, the purge_unreachable method will raise a RuntimeError exception if it tries to alter the array referenced by the NETWORKS constant. As a general rule of thumb, always freeze constants to prevent them from being mutated. Unfortunately, freezing the NETWORKS array isn't quite enough. Consider this:

```ruby
def host_addresses (host, networks=Defaults::NETWORKS)
  networks.map {|net| net << ".#{host}"}
end
```

The host_addresses method will modify the elements of the NETWORKS array if it isn't given a second argument. While the NETWORKS array itself is frozen, its *elements* are still mutable. You might not be able to add or remove elements from the array, but you can surely make changes to the existing elements. So, if a constant references a collection object such as an array or hash, freeze the collection *and* its elements:

```ruby
module Defaults
  NETWORKS = [
    "192.168.1",
    "192.168.2",
  ].map!(&:freeze).freeze
end
```

(If you happen to be using Ruby 2.1 or later you can make use of a trick from Item 47 and freeze the string literals directly. This can save you a bit of memory while keeping the elements from accidentally being mutated.)

Freezing a constant will change an obscure, hard-to-track-down bug into an exception. That's an obvious win. Unfortunately, it's still not enough. Even if you freeze the object a constant refers to, you can still cause problems by assigning a *new* value to an existing constant. See for yourself:

```
irb> TIMEOUT = 5
---> 5

irb> TIMEOUT += 5
(irb):2: warning: already initialized constant TIMEOUT
(irb):1: warning: previous definition of TIMEOUT was here
---> 10
```

As you can see, assigning a new value to an existing constant is perfectly legal in Ruby. You can also see that Ruby produces a warning telling us that we're redefining a constant. But that's it, just a warning. Thankfully, if we take things into our own hands, we can make Ruby raise an exception if we accidentally redefine a constant. The solution is a bit clumsy, and may be too heavy-handed for some situations, but it's simple. To prevent Ruby from assigning new values to existing constants, freeze the class or module they're defined in. You may even want to structure your code so that all constants are defined in their own module, isolating the effects of the freeze method:

```
module Defaults
  TIMEOUT = 5
end

Defaults.freeze
```

There are three levels of freezing you should consider when defining constants. The first two are easy: freeze the object that the constant references and the module the constant is defined in. Those two steps prevent the constant from being mutated or assigned to. The third is a bit more complicated. We saw that if a constant references an array of strings, we need to freeze the array *and* the elements. In other words, you need to deeply freeze the object the constant refers to. Each constant will be different, just make sure it's completely frozen.

Things to Remember

✦ Always freeze constants to prevent them from being mutated.

✦ If a constant references a collection object such as an array or hash, freeze the collection *and* its elements.

✦ To prevent assignment of new values to existing constants, freeze the module they're defined in.

Item 5: Pay Attention to Run-Time Warnings

Ruby programmers enjoy a shortened feedback loop while writing, executing, and testing code. Being interpreted, the compilation phase isn't present in Ruby. Or is it? If you think about it, Ruby must do some of the same things a compiler does, such as parsing our source code. When you give your Ruby code to the interpreter, it has to perform some compiler-like tasks before it starts to execute the code. It's useful to think about Ruby working with our code in two phases: compile time and run time.

Parsing and making sense of our code happens at compile time. Executing that code happens at run time. This distinction is especially important when you consider the various types of warnings that Ruby can produce. Warnings emitted during the compilation phase usually have something to do with syntax problems that Ruby was able to work around. Run-time warnings, on the other hand, can indicate sloppy programming that might be the source of potential bugs. Paying attention to these warnings can help you fix mistakes before they become real problems. Before we talk about how to enable the various warnings in Ruby, let's explore a few of the common warning messages and what causes them.

Warnings emitted during the compilation phase are especially important to pay attention to. The majority of them are generated when Ruby encounters ambiguous syntax and proceeds by choosing one of many possible interpretations. You obviously don't want Ruby guessing what you really meant. Imagine what would happen if a future version of Ruby changed its interpretation of ambiguous code and your program started behaving differently! By paying attention to these types of warnings you can make the necessary changes to your code and completely avoid the ambiguity in the first place. Here's an example of where the code isn't completely clear and Ruby produces a warning:

```
irb> "808".split /0/
warning: ambiguous first argument; put parentheses or even spaces
```

When Ruby's parser reaches the first forward slash, it has to decide if it's the beginning of a regular expression literal, or if it's the division operator. In this case, it makes the reasonable assumption that the slash starts a regular expression and should be the first argument to the split method. But it's not hard to see how it could also be interpreted as the division operator with the output of the split command being its left operand. The warning itself is generic, and only half of it is helpful. But the fix is simple enough—use parentheses:

```
irb> "808".split(/0/)
---> ["8", "8"]
```

If you send your code through Ruby with warnings enabled you're likely to see other warnings related to operators and parentheses. The reason is nearly always the same. Ruby isn't 100% sure what you mean and picks the most reasonable interpretation. But again, do you really want Ruby guessing what you mean or would you rather be completely clear from the start? Here are two more examples of ambiguous method calls that are fixed by adding parentheses around the arguments:

```
irb> dirs = ['usr', 'local', 'bin']

irb> File.join *dirs
warning: '*' interpreted as argument prefix

irb> File.join(*dirs)
---> "usr/local/bin"

irb> dirs.map &:length
warning: '&' interpreted as argument prefix

irb> dirs.map(&:length)
---> [3, 5, 3]
```

Other useful warnings during the compilation phase have to do with variables. For example, Ruby will warn you if you assign a value to a variable, but then never end up using it. This might mean you're wasting a bit of memory but could also mean you've forgotten to include a value in your calculation. You'll also receive a warning if you create two variables with the same name in the same scope, so-called *variable shadowing*. This can happen if you accidentally specify a block argument with the same name as a variable that's already in scope. Both types of variable warnings can be seen in this example:

```
irb> def add (x, y)
       z = 1
       x + y
     end
warning: assigned but unused variable - z

irb> def repeat (n, &block)
       n.times {|n| block.call(n)}
     end
warning: shadowing outer local variable - n
```

As you can see, these compile-time warnings don't necessarily mean that you've done anything wrong, but they certainly *could* mean that.

So the best course of action is to review the warnings and make changes to your source code accordingly. The same can also be said of warnings generated while your code is executing, or what I call run-time warnings. These are warnings that can only be detected after your code has done something suspicious such as accessing an uninitialized instance variable or redefining an existing method. Both of which could have been done on purpose or by accident. Like the other warnings we've seen, these are easy to remedy.

I think you get the point, so I won't enumerate a bunch of descriptive, easy-to-fix run-time warnings for you. Instead, I'd rather show you how to enable warnings in the first place. Here again, it becomes important to distinguish between compile time and run time. If you want Ruby to produce warnings about your code as it's being parsed, you need to make sure the interpreter's warning flag is enabled. That might be as easy as passing the "-w" command-line option to Ruby:

```
ruby -w script.rb
```

For some types of applications, it's not that simple. Perhaps your Ruby program is being started automatically by a web server or a background job processing server. More commonly, you're using something like Rake to run your tests and you want warnings enabled. When you can't enable warnings by giving the interpreter the "-w" command-line option, you can do it indirectly by setting the RUBYOPT environment variable. How you set this variable will depend on the operating system and how your application is being started. What's most important is that the RUBYOPT environment variable be set to "-w" within the environment where your application is going to run *before* Ruby starts.

(I should also mention that if you're using Rake to run your tests you have another option available for enabling warnings. Item 36 includes an example Rakefile that does just that.)

Now, there's one last way to enable warnings. It's poorly documented and as a result often causes a lot of confusion. Within your program you can inspect and manipulate the $VERBOSE global variable (and its alias, $-w). If you want all possible warning messages you should set this variable to true. Setting it to false lowers the verbosity (producing fewer warnings) and setting it to nil disables warnings altogether. You might be thinking to yourself, "Hey, if I can set $VERBOSE to true, then I don't need to mess around with this '-w' business." This is where the distinction between compile time and run time really helps.

If you don't use the "-w" command-line option with the Ruby interpreter, but instead rely upon the $VERBOSE variable, you won't be able to see compile-time warnings. That's because setting the $VERBOSE global variable doesn't happen until your program is *running*. By that time, the parsing phase is over and you've missed all the compile-time warnings. So, there are two guidelines to follow. First, enable compile-time warnings by using the "-w" command-line option to the Ruby interpreter or by setting the RUBYOPT environment variable to "-w". Second, control run-time warnings using the $VERBOSE global variable.

My advice is to always enable compile-time *and* run-time warnings during application development and while tests are running. If you absolutely must disable run-time warnings, do so by temporarily setting the $VERBOSE global variable to nil.

Unfortunately, enabling warning messages comes with a warning of its own. I'm disappointed to report that it's not common practice to enable warnings. So, if you're using any RubyGems and enable warnings, you're likely to get *a lot* of warnings originating from within them. This may strongly tempt you to subsequently disable warnings. Thankfully, when Ruby prints warnings to the terminal it includes the file name and line number corresponding to the warning. It shouldn't be too hard for you to write a script to filter out unwanted warnings. Even better, become a good open-source citizen and contribute fixes for any gems that are being a little sloppy and producing warnings.

Things to Remember

+ Use the "-w" command-line option to the Ruby interpreter to enable compile-time and run-time warnings. You can also set the RUBYOPT environment variable to "-w".

+ If you must disable run-time warnings, do so by temporarily setting the $VERBOSE global variable to nil.

Classes, Objects, and Modules

Object-oriented programming (OOP) is Ruby's bread and butter. It's often referred to as a purely object-oriented language because everything in Ruby is an object or can be turned into one, and I mean *everything*. From classes all the way down to numeric literals, Ruby exposes a consistent design that is found in few other languages.

Ruby's object model was heavily influenced by Smalltalk and is probably a bit different than what you're used to if you're coming from languages like C++ or Java. The fact that classes are also objects is enough to send your mind into infinite recursion if you let it. Then there are some gotchas like subclasses not automatically initializing their superclasses and the ambiguity between defining variables and calling setter methods. This chapter tackles these issues and sorts them all out.

Additionally, I'll explain the way Ruby actually builds inheritance hierarchies when you create classes, subclasses, and mix modules into them. Armed with this information you'll be able to track down how methods are introduced into your classes and where they came from, an important skill when dealing with large frameworks such as Ruby on Rails.

Understanding Ruby's flavor of OOP will help you make better decisions and avoid long-term design mistakes. Especially when it comes to Ruby's open and dynamic nature, which can be used to create leaky abstractions and ignore encapsulation. Both of which will lead to maintenance nightmares and late-night debugging sessions. Something I'll help you avoid.

Item 6: Know How Ruby Builds Inheritance Hierarchies

Question: When you send a message to an object, how does Ruby locate the appropriate method? The answer is deceptively simple: Using the inheritance hierarchy. This answer is deceptive because of the way in which Ruby constructs inheritance hierarchies behind the scenes. This is one of those rare situations where Ruby goes out of its way to obscure what's really going on under the covers, often leading to unnecessary confusion. The methods Ruby gives us for discovering which classes are part of a hierarchy don't always tell the whole truth. Fortunately, the way the Ruby interpreter internally builds the inheritance hierarchy is both consistent and straightforward once you understand a few of its tricks.

Exploring how Ruby searches for methods will provide some good insight into the language's implementation and give us the perfect environment for unraveling a class's true inheritance hierarchy. Something you should definitely be aware of. The good news is that by the end of this item you'll never be surprised by Ruby's object model again. The bad news is that we'll need to start by reviewing some classic OOP terminology and how a few general terms have specific definitions in Ruby. Bear with me for a few paragraphs.

- An *object* is a container of variables. These variables are referred to as *instance variables* and represent the state of an object. Each object has a special, internal variable that connects it to one and only one class. Because of this connection the object is said to be an *instance* of this class.

- A *class* is a container of methods and constants. The methods are referred to as *instance methods* and represent the behavior for all objects that are instances of the class.

  Things get a little confusing and circular here because classes are themselves objects. So, each class is also a container of variables called *class variables*. These *class objects*, like all other objects, have methods. Technically, these methods are indistinguishable from instance methods but to avoid excessive confusion they are called *class methods*. In other words, classes are objects whose variables are called class variables and whose methods are called class methods. (Class objects can also have instance variables, but we'll get to that in Item 15.)

- A *superclass* is a fancy name for the parent class in a class hierarchy. If class B inherits from class A, then A is the superclass of B. Classes have special, internal variables to keep track of their superclasses.

- A *module* is identical to a class in all respects but one. So like classes, modules are objects and are instances of a particular class. While classes are instances of the Class class, modules are instances of the Module class. Internally, Ruby implements modules and classes using the same data structure but limits what you can do with them through their class methods (there's no new method) and a more restrictive syntax.

Modules have many uses in Ruby but for now we're only concerned with how they contribute to the inheritance hierarchy. Although Ruby doesn't directly support multiple inheritance, modules can be mixed into a class with the include method, which has a similar effect.

- A *singleton class* is a confusing term for an anonymous and invisible class in the inheritance hierarchy.

The confusion around these classes doesn't necessarily come from their purpose as much as it does from their name. They are sometimes referred to as eigenclasses or metaclasses. Even the source code for the Ruby interpreter uses these terms interchangeably. In this book I'll always refer to them as singleton classes since that's the name you'll see within Ruby when working with the introspection methods such as singleton_class and singleton_methods.

Singleton classes play an important role in Ruby, such as providing a place to store class methods and methods included from modules. Unlike other classes, they're created dynamically on an as-needed basis by Ruby itself. They also come with restrictions. For example, you can't create an instance of a singleton class. The only thing you really need to remember here is that singleton classes are just regular classes that don't have names and are subjected to a couple of limitations.

- A *receiver* is the object on which a method is invoked. For example, in "customer.name" the method invoked is name and the receiver is customer. While the name method is executing, the self variable is set to customer and any instance variables accessed will come from the customer object. Sometimes the receiver is omitted from method calls, in which case it's implicitly set to whatever self is in the current context.

Phew! Now that we're done with the vocabulary lesson we can explore Ruby's object model and how it constructs inheritance hierarchies. Let's start by putting together a small class hierarchy and use IRB to play with it:

```
class Person
  def name
    . . .
```

```
  end
end

class Customer < Person
  ...
end
irb> customer = Customer.new
---> #<Customer>

irb> customer.class
---> Customer

irb> Customer.superclass
---> Person

irb> customer.respond_to?(:name)
---> true
```

There's nothing too surprising in this code. If you invoke the name method on the customer object the method lookup will happen exactly as you expect. First, the Customer class would be checked for a matching instance method. It's obviously not there so the search would continue up the inheritance hierarchy to the Person class where it would be found and executed. If the method hadn't been found there Ruby would continue searching all the way up until either it was found or it hit the root class, BasicObject. You can see the complete hierarchy in Figure 2-1.

As you know, if the method lookup makes it all the way to the root of the class tree without finding a match it will restart the search where it began, this time looking for the method_missing method. Item 30 asks you to consider alternatives to defining your own method_missing method so we won't cover it here. That is, other than to say there's a default implementation of method_missing in the Kernel module that raises an exception to punish you for calling an undefined method.

Which reminds me: It's time to take this simple example and throw a wrench into it:

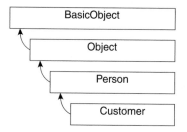

Figure 2-1 Customer class inheritance hierarchy.

```ruby
module ThingsWithNames
  def name
    ...
  end
end

class Person
  include(ThingsWithNames)
end
irb> Person.superclass
---> Object

irb> customer = Customer.new
---> #<Customer>

irb> customer.respond_to?(:name)
---> true
```

I've taken the name method out of the Person class and moved it into a module that is then included in the Person class. Instances of the Customer class still respond to the name method as you'd expect, but why? Clearly, the ThingsWithNames module isn't in the inheritance hierarchy because the superclass of Person is still Object, or is it? As it turns out this is where Ruby starts to lie to you and where we need to talk about singleton classes a bit more.

When you use the include method to mix in a module Ruby is doing something very sneaky behind the scenes. It creates a singleton class and inserts it into the class hierarchy. This anonymous and invisible class is linked to the module so they share instance methods and constants. In the case of the Person class, when it includes the ThingsWithNames module, Ruby creates a singleton class and silently inserts it as the superclass of Person. "But calling the superclass method on Person returns Object, not ThingsWithNames," you say. Yep, and for good reason: The singleton class is *anonymous* and *invisible* so both the superclass and class methods skip over it. So, a more accurate class hierarchy needs to include modules too. And that's exactly what Figure 2-2 contains.

As each module is included into a class it is inserted into the hierarchy immediately above the including class in a last in, first out (LIFO) manner. Everything is connected through the superclass variable like a singly linked list. The net result is that when Ruby is searching for a method it will visit each module in reverse order, most recently included first. An important point to take away from this is that modules can never override methods from the class that includes them. Since modules are inserted above the including class Ruby always checks the class before moving upward. (Okay...this isn't entirely

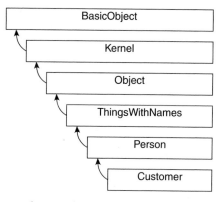

Figure 2-2 Customer class inheritance hierarchy with modules.

true. Be sure to read Item 35 to see how the prepend method in Ruby 2.0 complicates this.)

Now that you're comfortable with the interaction between modules and singleton classes it's my duty to shake things up and introduce yet another weird (but lovely) wrench in the works:

```
customer = Customer.new

def customer.name
  "Leonard"
end
```

If you haven't seen this syntax before it can be a little confusing at first, but it's actually pretty straightforward. The code above defines a method that exists only for this one object—customer. This specific method cannot be called on any other object. How do you suppose Ruby implements that? If you're pointing a finger at singleton classes you'd be correct. In fact, this method is called a *singleton method*. When Ruby executes this code it will create a singleton class, install the name method as an instance method, and then insert this anonymous class as the class of the customer object. Even though the class of the customer object is now a singleton class, the introspective class method in Ruby will skip over it and still return Customer. This obscures things for us but makes life easier for Ruby. When it searches for the name method it only needs to traverse the class hierarchy. No special logic is needed.

This should also shed some light on why these kinds of classes are known as singleton classes. Most classes service many objects. The Array class, for example, contains the methods for every array object used in your program. Singleton classes, on the other hand, only serve a single object.

With no more tricks up my sleeve I'm left with only class methods to describe. You'll be pleasantly surprised to know that you probably already understand them. They're another form of the singleton method we just explored.

Notice that when you define a singleton method you specify an object (almost like it's the receiver), which will be the owner of the method. When you define a class method you do the exact same thing by specifying the class object, either through the class's name or more commonly by using the self variable. An object is an object after all, even if that object is a class. So class methods are stored as instance methods on a singleton class. See for yourself:

```
class Customer < Person
  def self.where_am_i?
    ...
  end
end
irb> Customer.singleton_class.instance_methods(false)
---> [:where_am_i?]

irb> Customer.singleton_class.superclass
---> #<Class:Person>
```

In the end, when Ruby wants to look up a method, it only has to consider the inheritance hierarchy. This works for both instance methods and class methods. Once you understand how Ruby manipulates the inheritance hierarchy the process for looking up a method is pretty easy:

1. Get the class of the receiver, which may actually be a hidden singleton class. (Remember that you can't actually do this from Ruby code because the class method skips over singleton classes. You'd have to go straight to the singleton_class method.)

2. Search the list of instance methods that are stored in the class. If the method is found stop searching and execute the method. Otherwise, continue to step 3.

3. Move up the hierarchy to the superclass and repeat step 2. (Again, the superclass may actually be another singleton class. From within Ruby—the superclass method specifically—it would be invisible.)

4. Steps 2 and 3 are repeated until Ruby finds the method or reaches the top of the hierarchy.

5. When it reaches the top, Ruby starts back at step 1 with the original receiver, but this time looking for the method_missing method.

As you can see, when methods are stored in invisible singleton classes it's not as straightforward to see the entire hierarchy from within the code. But you can piece together the real picture using a handful of methods that Ruby provides for introspection purposes.

- The `singleton_class` method returns the singleton class for the receiver, creating it if it doesn't already exist.

- The `ancestors` method returns an array of all the classes and modules that make up the inheritance hierarchy. It can only be called on classes or modules and skips over singleton classes.

- The `included_modules` method returns the same array as ancestors with the exception that all the classes have been filtered out.

Thankfully, you'll rarely need to use these methods. Knowing how the inheritance hierarchy is constructed and searched internally is enough to clarify most situations. That said, Item 35 includes a few examples just in case.

Things to Remember

- ✦ To find a method, Ruby only has to search up the class hierarchy. If it doesn't find the method it's looking for it starts the search again, trying to find the `method_missing` method.

- ✦ Including modules silently creates singleton classes that are inserted into the hierarchy above the including class.

- ✦ Singleton methods (class methods and per-object methods) are stored in singleton classes that are also inserted into the hierarchy.

Item 7: Be Aware of the Different Behaviors of super

Suppose you've written a class that inherits from a base class. This base class defines a method that, in the context of your class, doesn't quite do everything you need it to. So you've decided to improve the method. But you don't want to completely replace the existing method since it already performs 90% of the necessary heavy lifting. You also don't want to change the base class because that would break other code. Ignoring the fact that composition might be a better choice than inheritance, you plow ahead and override the method. You wind up with something like this:

```
class Base
  def m1 (x, y)
    ...
  end
end
```

```
class Derived < Base
  def m1 (x)
    # How do you call Base#m1?
  end
end
```

You've gotten yourself into a pickle. The big question is: How do you call the version of m1 that exists in the superclass? If you try calling m1 from the Derived class you'll just go into infinite recursion. That's not going to help much. This is where super comes in:

```
def m1 (x)
  super(x, x)
  ...
end
```

Now we're getting somewhere. This version of m1 uses super to invoke its parent's copy of m1, the one from the Base class. In this case, super sort of stands in for Base#m1. You can use super in any way you'd use Base#m1 directly. This includes passing whichever arguments you want to the Base copy of m1 through super. (Just as long as the target method accepts those arguments.) This creates a subtle illusion that can bite you if you're not careful.

Even though super is used and acts like a method, it's actually a language keyword. This difference is important because super changes its behavior based on something that is supposed to be optional in Ruby—parentheses. Seriously, think about that for a second. Choosing to omit parentheses when using super changes the way it works. It's even slightly worse than it sounds. To see how parentheses change things we'll need to review the three ways that super can be written:

- The first way of using super is the least surprising—it's the way we've been using it so far. If you give super at least one argument then it acts like a regular Ruby method and the parentheses are optional. In this form, super passes along the exact arguments it was given to the target method.

- If no arguments are given *and* no parentheses are used super will act in a way you might not expect. Used this way, super will invoke the target method with *all* of the arguments that were given to the enclosing method. It also forwards along the method's block if one is associated with it.

  There are a couple of side effects with this form of super that you should watch out for. First, using super this way only works if the target method accepts the same number of arguments as the enclosing method. As an example, this wouldn't be the case for the Base#m1 and Derived#m1 methods we looked at earlier. Trying to use super with no arguments in Derived#m1 would result in an ArgumentError exception. You'll be bitten by the same exception if the overridden method doesn't expect any arguments but the enclosing method does.

The second thing to watch out for has to do with the value of the arguments given to the overridden method. If you mutate one of the enclosing method's arguments before calling super with no arguments, super will pass their current value to the target method, not their original values. This seems pretty reasonable but something you need to be aware of.

- When you don't actually want to pass any arguments to the overridden method you need to write super with an empty set of parentheses, i.e., super(). This looks especially weird in Ruby. Even those of us who prefer to use parentheses don't do so when calling a method with no arguments. This use of super seems unnatural, but it's the only way to call an overridden method with no arguments (and no block).

Here are the same rules from above expressed in code:

```ruby
class SuperSilliness < SillyBase
  def m1 (x, y)
    super(1, 2) # Call with 1, 2.
    super(x, y) # Call with x, y.
    super x, y  # Same as above.
    super       # Same as above.
    super()     # Call without arguments.
  end
end
```

The next thing we need to concern ourselves with is how super goes about finding the overridden method. It would appear that super simply calls the superclass's copy of the current method, but that's an oversimplification. In reality, super considers the entire inheritance hierarchy and follows the rules laid out in Item 6, but with a minor change. When you use super it searches for a method with the same name as the current method, just higher up in the inheritance hierarchy. So, it needs to start at the next level up and continue from there.

If you remember our study of the inheritance hierarchy you'll know that the next level up might be a singleton class. This is great because it means that super can be used to access overridden methods from included modules. For example:

```
module CoolFeatures
  def feature_a
    ...
  end
end
class Vanilla
  include(CoolFeatures)

  def feature_a
    ...
    super # CoolFeatures#feature_a
  end
end
```

This example also points out a limitation when using super. If you want to reach a method that is defined in a superclass and an included module also defines a method with the same name, super won't work. Obviously, super is going to stop at the first matching method it finds, which would be in the module, not the superclass. But if you happen to run into this situation you've probably made a serious design error. Consider using composition instead of inheritance.

Finally, the last thing I want to warn you about is how super interacts with method_missing. If you think about it, as long as you only ever use super in a method that has the same name as another method in the inheritance hierarchy it won't involve method_missing. On the other hand, if you're an especially sleepy driver or doing some sort of voodoo metaprogramming you might wind up with a call to super that eventually invokes method_missing. In that case, you'll be glad you read this section.

As with the normal method lookup, if super can't find the method it's looking for it will call method_missing to report the error. As you'd expect, Ruby starts its search for method_missing with the class of the original receiver. All this is fine and good, and we even get a useful error message from the resulting exception:

```
class SuperHappy
  def laugh
    super
    ...
  end
end
irb> SuperHappy.new.laugh
NoMethodError: super: no superclass method 'laugh' for
#<SuperHappy>
```

Internally, Ruby tracks whether or not method_missing is being invoked due to a bad super call and provides an extra bit of information along with the exception. But this only works if Ruby doesn't find any definition of method_missing in the inheritance hierarchy and therefore uses the default implementation. Once *any* class in the hierarchy defines a method_missing method you'll lose this useful detail. There's no way to get it back, even if you make it a point to call super from within your implementation of method_missing.

Furthermore, method_missing will be invoked with details about a method that actually *does* exist, just in the wrong place. If the SuperHappy class above defined a method_missing method it would get invoked when we call laugh because that method tries to use super to call another copy of itself, which doesn't exist. And what's the first argument to method_missing? That's right, it's the name of the missing method, which in this case would be :laugh. But SuperHappy does have a laugh method. Confusing, huh?

If you're counting reasons to avoid defining a method_missing method, make sure to include this one too (along with those mentioned in Item 30). In this case, the NoMethodError exception from the default implementation of method_missing is demonstrably better than anything we could do in our own method_missing.

Things to Remember

+ When you override a method from the inheritance hierarchy the super keyword can be used to call the overridden method.

+ Using super with no arguments and no parentheses is equivalent to passing it all of the arguments that were given to the enclosing method.

+ If you want to use super without passing the overridden method any arguments, you must use empty parentheses, i.e., super().

+ Defining a method_missing method will discard helpful information when a super call fails. See Item 30 for alternatives to method_missing.

Item 8: Invoke super When Initializing Subclasses

In Ruby, classes don't have traditional OOP-style constructors. If we're interested in controlling the initial state of our objects we need to write a method named initialize and do the necessary work there. This method is called by new just after a new object has been freshly allocated. If you don't write your own initialize method your class will inherit the default implementation from the BasicObject class. But it's not all that useful. In fact, it's an empty method that doesn't do anything at all. It's only there so new has something to call if you don't define your own version of initialize. Fortunately, there are plenty of times when BasicObject#initialize will suit your needs just fine. But when you do need to define an initialize method there's a slight catch.

It's easy to forget that initialize is just a regular old private instance method so it follows all the normal method lookup rules. For example, if you wanted, you could define a reset method that simply called initialize to reset all instance variables to their initial states. But the choice to treat initialize as a regular method comes with a surprising consequence. When you write an initialize method you also override all other definitions of initialize that are higher up in the inheritance hierarchy. If you're used to a language that has official constructors you might expect all the methods in the hierarchy to be chained together instead of overriding one another. That's not the case in Ruby. Consider this:

```ruby
class Parent
  attr_accessor(:name)

  def initialize
    @name = "Howard"
  end
end
class Child < Parent
  attr_accessor(:grade)

  def initialize
    @grade = 8
  end
end
```

Looking at Parent#initialize, it's clear that if you create a new Parent object the @name instance variable will be initialized with a default value. It's also clear from Child#initialize that creating a new Child object will set up a @grade instance variable. The potentially unclear question is whether creating a Child object would also result in @name being set. Playing with the code in IRB clears things up:

```
irb> adult = Parent.new
---> #<Parent @name="Howard">

irb> youngster = Child.new
---> #<Child @grade=8>

irb> youngster.name
---> nil
```

Ouch. Ruby doesn't automatically call overridden methods, not even `initialize`. In this case the `initialize` method in the `Parent` class isn't called when using `Child::new` because the `Child` class has its own `initialize` method that overrides the one from `Parent`. Rewriting these `initialize` methods to take arguments will make this even clearer.

```
class Parent
  def initialize (name)
    @name = name
  end
end
class Child < Parent
  def initialize (grade)
    @grade = grade
  end
end
```

Now you can see the dilemma. Ruby doesn't provide a way for us to specify the relationship between an `initialize` method in a subclass and the one from its superclass. So it has no way of knowing how to automatically call `initialize` in a superclass and pass the correct arguments. So it doesn't and leaves the task to us. This can be surprising to new Ruby programmers and something even experienced programmers forget.

Since Ruby doesn't initialize parent classes for us, how do we do it ourselves? The solution comes from the fact that `initialize` is just like any other overridden method. That is, we can use the general-purpose `super` keyword to call a method with the same name higher up in the hierarchy.

```
class Child < Parent
  def initialize (name, grade)
    super(name) # Initialize Parent.
    @grade = grade
  end
end
irb> youngster = Child.new("Abigail", 8)
---> #<Child @name="Abigail", @grade=8>

irb> youngster.name
---> "Abigail"
```

What we lose in automatic construction behavior we gain in flexibility. Using `super` in the `initialize` methods of subclasses gives us fine-grained control over how and when we initialize superclasses. Should the superclass be initialized before the subclass? Do we need to set some instance variables before initializing superclasses? We're free to mix and match behaviors as we see fit. Just make sure you remember to use super and take a moment to review some of its quirks, which are discussed in Item 7.

Before we wrap up here I should remind you that initialize isn't the only way to set up a new object. Ruby lets us create copies of objects using the dup and clone methods. When you use one of these methods the newly created copy is given a chance to perform any special copying logic by defining an initialize_copy method. If you override the initialize_copy method from a superclass you'll definitely want to use super to let it set itself up correctly.

Things to Remember

+ Ruby doesn't automatically call the initialize method in a superclass when creating objects from a subclass. Instead, normal method lookup rules apply to initialize and only the first matching copy is invoked.

+ When writing an initialize method for a class that explicitly uses inheritance, use super to initialize the parent class. The same rule applies when you define an initialize_copy method.

Item 9: Be Alert for Ruby's Most Vexing Parse

When it comes to method-naming rules, Ruby gives us a lot of freedom. While not as liberal as languages such as Lisp, Ruby does let us use one of three nonalphanumeric characters at the end of method names: "?", "!", and "=". Two of those characters are purely aesthetic but one of them has special meaning to Ruby.

As you know, tacking a question mark on the end of a method name doesn't change anything about the method nor does it make Ruby treat it any differently. It's merely a naming convention adopted by Ruby programmers to indicate that a method returns a Boolean value. (Or what Ruby considers to be a Boolean value. See Item 1 for details.) This naming convention isn't enforced and methods ending in "?" can still return whatever value they want. The exclamation point is similar, if not just a bit more vague. It usually means that the method will mutate the receiver but can also warn you about a potentially harmful action. Both are loose guidelines that Ruby programmers tend to follow. Ending a method name with an equal sign, on the other hand, is something entirely different.

Appending "=" to the end of a method's name turns it into a *setter* method and allows you to invoke that method with some nifty syntax. Typically, such methods take a single argument, update some internal state, and return their argument. This means that setter methods can also be used as lvalues (the left-hand side of an assignment).

```ruby
class SetMe
  def initialize
    @value = 0
  end

  def value # "Getter"
    @value
  end

  def value= (x) # "Setter"
    @value = x
  end
end
irb> x = SetMe.new
---> #<SetMe @value=0>

irb> x.value = 1 # Call setter.
---> 1

irb> x
---> #<SetMe @value=1>
```

Even though "=" is technically part of the method's name, Ruby lets us place whitespace between it and the rest of the name. It looks like variable assignment, but it's actually just a plain old method call. You can see this more clearly when you add parentheses and remove the whitespace.

```ruby
irb> x.value=(1)
---> 1
```

You may have never defined one of these setter methods by hand but you've definitely done it indirectly. That's because Ruby has helper methods that write them for us. Both attr_writer and attr_accessor define setter methods that are exactly like the value= example above. The indirection can be confusing, which is why I bring them up. As long as you remember what these helper methods do, and the advice that follows, you'll steer clear of any trouble.

Speaking of trouble, we need to consider the ambiguity between assignments and setters. Because setter method invocation looks just like variable assignment it's easy to confuse the two. Consider this:

```ruby
class Counter
  attr_accessor(:counter)

  def initialize
    counter = 0
  end
  ...
end
```

It's not unreasonable to assume that the body of the `initialize` method is calling the `counter=` method, and it's an assumption that a lot of people make. But it's not correct, of course; it's just a simple variable assignment. The `initialize` method creates a new local variable called `counter`, sets it to 0, and then throws away the reference to it when the scope ends. Not at all what we wanted to do but obvious when you think about it. (And if you have warnings enabled as recommeded in Item 5, Ruby will tell you when you make this mistake.)

There's a parsing ambiguity between variable assignment and calling setter methods. Ruby resolves it by requiring that setter methods be called with an *explicit receiver*. In order to invoke a setter method instead of creating a variable you need to prepend a receiver to the method name. So, to call the `counter=` method from within an instance method you need to use `self` as the receiver.

```ruby
class Counter
  attr_accessor(:counter)

  def initialize
    self.counter = 0
  end
  ...
end
```

With `self` used as the receiver Ruby will parse our code correctly and invoke the `counter=` setter method instead of creating a new variable. You might think that you could avoid using `self` if you invoked the method with no whitespace and used parentheses (i.e., `counter=(0)`) but that doesn't work either. We're stuck with using `self` as an explicit receiver, which leads to another problem.

Programmers bitten by this parsing rule tend to overcompensate by littering their code with unnecessary `self` receivers. While there's nothing technically wrong with putting `self` in front of every method call, it sure is ugly. It's a matter of taste for sure, but one that is fairly

universal among Ruby programmers. See if you can spot the unnecessary uses of self in the following code:

```
class Name
  attr_accessor(:first, :last)

  def initialize (first, last)
    self.first = first
    self.last  = last
  end

  def full
    self.first + " " + self.last
  end
end
```

Clearly, the full method is using self redundantly. With no setter
methods involved you can safely remove the use of self and rely on
some simple parsing rules. When Ruby comes across an identifier like
first or last it checks to see if there's a variable in the current scope
with a matching name. When it doesn't find one it tries to look up
the identifier as a method. In the case of the two attributes from the
Name class, Ruby finds the getter methods defined by the earlier use of
attr_accessor. Here's another version of the full method that does the
same thing as before but with less noise:

```
def full
  first + " " + last
end
```

At this point, there should be no doubt in your mind that setter methods are a special kind of animal. If you don't want any surprises
remember to call them with a receiver. But don't let that fool you into
thinking that all methods need receivers, especially when called from
within instances methods. For every other type of method, Ruby will
automatically use self as the receiver if the method call is missing it.

Things to Remember

+ Setter methods can only be called with an explicit receiver. Without
  a receiver they will be parsed as variable assignments.

+ When invoking a setter method from within an instance method
  use self as the receiver.

+ You don't need to use an explicit receiver when calling nonsetter
  methods. In other words, don't litter your code with self.

Item 10: Prefer Struct to Hash for Structured Data

Hash tables are very useful, general-purpose data structures that are employed heavily by Ruby programmers. The Hash class provides a simple interface for working with hash tables and is such a big part of Ruby that, like arrays, it has its own dedicated syntax for creating new instances. When it comes to working with key-value pairs, Hash is definitely the go-to class.

In fact, Ruby programmers use hashes all the time. Even method keyword arguments are implemented with the Hash class and a pinch of syntactic sugar. They're so general that hashes can be used to emulate types such as arrays, sets, and even basic objects. When working with structured data in an OOP language we often have better choices than hashes, and Ruby is no exception. Let's look at a typical use of the Hash class and then consider replacing it with something more appropriate.

Say you're interested in exploring annual weather data from a local weather station. Armed with a CSV file from the National Oceanic and Atmospheric Administration (NOAA) you plan to load the data into an array and play around with it. Each row in the CSV file contains temperature statistics for a single month. You've decided to extract the interesting columns from each row and store them in a Hash. Consider this:

```ruby
require('csv')
class AnnualWeather
  def initialize (file_name)
    @readings = []

    CSV.foreach(file_name, headers: true) do |row|
      @readings << {
        :date => Date.parse(row[2]),
        :high => row[10].to_f,
        :low  => row[11].to_f,
      }
    end
  end
end
```

There's nothing out of the ordinary here. Each row read from the CSV file is transformed into a hash that is then inserted into an array. After the initialize method is complete you'll have an array of uniform hashes, that is, all of the hashes will have the same keys but different values. Essentially this array of hashes represents a collection of objects, except that you can't access their attributes through getter methods. You have to use the hash index operator instead. This might be a minor issue but it's one that will have an impact on the AnnualWeather class's interface.

You shouldn't allow this array of hashes to leak through the public interface because the keys for each hash are an internal implementation detail. Without class-level documentation, other programmers would have to read the entire definition of the initialize method to know which keys are populated with which CSV columns. It might not be much of a burden when initialize is the only method that is setting keys, but as the class matures this may no longer be the case. This is a weakness when using hashes to emulate objects and one that isn't limited to the public interface.

Every time you want to work with these hashes internally you will need to go back to the initialize method to remind yourself of which keys are available. Again, as long as the keys are set in a single method the burden is fairly low. Let's consider a situation where you're tempted to create a new key. Each month in the @readings array has high and low temperatures. You'd like to know the mean temperature of the year, which means you'll also need to know the mean temperature for each month.

```
def mean
  return 0.0 if @readings.size.zero?

  total = @readings.reduce(0.0) do |sum, reading|
    sum + (reading[:high] + reading[:low]) / 2.0
  end

  total / @readings.size.to_f
end
```

Calculating the mean temperature for each month is pretty simple. Even so, it would be better if each object in the @readings array responded to a mean method so you could abstract away the logic. It's possible to shoehorn such a method onto each of the hashes, but at that point the code would be needlessly obscure. (We're not working in JavaScript after all.)

Using hashes to stand in for really simple classes tends to happen a lot in Ruby. Sometimes it's completely fine, but more often than not we really should be creating dedicated types for these kinds of objects. If you're lazy like me, the thought of creating a new class for something so simple seems like an unnecessary chore. Fortunately, that's exactly what the Struct class is for.

On the surface, using the Struct class is a lot like creating a new struct type in C++. But if you dig deeper you'll see that it's actually more like a class generator than a data structure. Using Struct is simple and only requires a call to the Struct::new method with a list of attributes. The return value from this method is virtually identical to a new class, which has getter and setter methods for each of the attributes. This new class also has an initialize method that accepts initial values for each of the attributes and sets them accordingly.

To replace the hashes we've been using so far we only need to make some minor changes to the initialize method.

```ruby
class AnnualWeather
  # Create a new struct to hold reading data.
  Reading = Struct.new(:date, :high, :low)

  def initialize (file_name)
    @readings = []

    CSV.foreach(file_name, headers: true) do |row|
      @readings << Reading.new(Date.parse(row[2]),
                               row[10].to_f,
                               row[11].to_f)
    end
  end
end
```

As you can see, it's common practice to assign the return value from the Struct::new method to a constant. This allows you to treat the constant like a class and create objects from it. This single line of code also makes it clear which methods you can expect objects of this new class to respond to. That's already a big improvement over the individual hashes. Let's see how this change affects the mean method:

```ruby
def mean
  return 0.0 if @readings.size.zero?

  total = @readings.reduce(0.0) do |sum, reading|
    sum + (reading.high + reading.low) / 2.0
  end

  total / @readings.size.to_f
end
```

This mean method required few changes but now has a much better OOP feel to it. Accessing the high and low attributes through getter methods has a subtle side effect too. Typos in attribute names will now raise a NoMethodError exception. This isn't the case when using hashes. Attempting to access an invalid key in a hash doesn't raise an exception but instead returns nil. This usually means you'll wind up with a more obscure TypeError exception later in the code. Another improvement with Struct is that we can now do something that we wanted to do earlier—define a mean method for each month.

The Struct class is more powerful than it first appears. In addition to a list of attributes, the Struct::new method can optionally take a block, which is then evaluated in the context of the new class. That's a mouthful, but it essentially means we can define instance and class methods inside the block. For example, here's how you'd define the mean method:

```ruby
Reading = Struct.new(:date, :high, :low) do
  def mean
    (high + low) / 2.0
  end
end
```

For those times when it seems too heavy-handed to create a new class, Struct can be very useful. And unlike a bunch of unrelated yet uniform hashes, Struct lets you define instance and class methods. That's perfect for when you need to add a few simple behaviors to these otherwise boring objects. They're also well typed with their own public interface, making them more suitable for users of the AnnualWeather class. The concern I had before about exposing an array of hashes through the AnnualWeather interface has been resolved, opening the way to an attr_reader for the @readings array. I'd say that's a big improvement.

Things to Remember

◆ When dealing with structured data which doesn't quite justify a new class prefer using Struct to Hash.

◆ Assign the return value of Struct::new to a constant and treat that constant like a class.

Item 11: Create Namespaces by Nesting Code in Modules

Imagine you're working on an application for ordering custom notebooks (the old fashioned paper kind). Customers can choose among many binding styles such as metal spirals or the more traditional glue. You decide to create a class to represent binding styles and all the options that go along with them. Unfortunately, things don't seem to be working as planned. What's wrong with the following class definition?

```ruby
class Binding
  def initialize (style, options={})
    @style = style
    @options = options
  end
end
```

At first glance everything seems to be correct. There are no syntax errors, but if you were to play with this class in IRB you'd see that something is really wrong. While the code above appears to create a new class, that's not actually what happens if you execute it. So if it doesn't define a class what does this code do? That's a mighty fine question.

As you know, classes in Ruby are mutable—you can add and replace methods at any time. The syntax for defining a class is the same syntax that is used to modify one. In this case, it just so happens that the class name you wanted to use has already been taken. Binding is a class in the Ruby core library. Instead of defining a new class the code above reopens and modifies an existing class. Not exactly what you had in mind.

Any nontrivial application is going to run into this problem sooner or later. It's an even bigger problem for library authors. What happens if more than one library defines the same class? How can you use both of the libraries at the same time? Thankfully, nearly every modern general-purpose programming language has a solution to this problem, including Ruby. The way we isolate our names from one another is done with a process called namespacing.

Namespaces are a way to qualify a constant so it becomes unique. At the most basic level namespaces let you create new scopes where you can define constants that would otherwise conflict with one another. Since class and module names are both constants, namespaces can be used to isolate them as well.

All of the core Ruby classes are said to be in the "global" namespace. We'll see what this actually means a bit later, but for now it's enough to know that each of these class names can be used without any sort of qualification. In other words, if you fire up IRB and type Array, what you mean is "the Array class in the global namespace." When you define a class without specifying a namespace you are placing that class into the global namespace. At the same time you're running the risk of clashing with an existing name.

Creating a new class and placing it into a custom namespace is as easy as nesting the class definition inside a module:

```ruby
module Notebooks
  class Binding
    ...
  end
end
```

Nesting the definition inside a module makes the Binding class distinct from, and avoids any confusion with, the core class of the same name. To reference this new class you need to include the module's name along with the "class path separator," which is two colons:

```
style = Notebooks::Binding.new
```

Using modules to create namespaces isn't limited to protecting classes; this technique can be used to place other constants and module functions inside namespaces as well. You can also nest modules within other modules to create arbitrarily deep namespaces. This is helpful in large applications and libraries as a way to keep code compartmentalized and modular.

When using namespaces it's common practice to mirror the namespace within the directory structure of the project on the file system. For example, under this scheme the class above would be found in the bindings.rb file located in a notebooks directory. In other words, the Notebooks::Bindings name maps to the notebooks/bindings.rb file.

Sometimes nesting classes in modules is cumbersome and causes unnecessary indentation. There's an alternative syntax for creating classes inside a namespace. It only works if the namespace already exists, that is, if the module that creates the namespace was previously defined. In this form you use the module name and class path separator directly in the class definition:

```
class Notebooks::Binding
   ...
end
```

Typically, you'd use this style of class definition by first defining the namespacing module in a main source file and then loading all remaining source files. But watch out. Attempting to use this syntax without first defining the namespace will result in a NameError exception. This is the exception Ruby raises if it can't find a referenced constant. Nesting constants inside one another adds some complexity to how you qualify the constants in your program, but understanding how Ruby searches for them will clear things up.

Ruby uses two techniques for finding constants. First, it examines the current lexical scope and all of the enclosing lexical scopes. (We'll explore lexical scopes shortly.) If the constant can't be found there Ruby searches the inheritance hierarchy. This is why you can use a constant defined in a superclass from within a subclass. As we'll see later, this is also why we can use the so-called "global" constants.

When dealing with namespaces we're mostly concerned with lexical scopes, the actual nested locations where a constant is defined or referenced. They're easier to see than read about so consider the following:

```ruby
module SuperDumbCrypto
  KEY = "password123"

  class Encrypt
    def initialize (key=KEY)
      ...
    end
  end
end
```

The module definition creates a lexical scope. Since the KEY constant *and* the Encrypt class are both defined in the same lexical scope the initialize method can use the KEY constant without qualifying it (i.e., giving the full class path to the constant). It's important to understand that the lexical scope is different from the namespace created by the module. It has to do with the physical location where the constants are defined and used. If we change things up a bit you can see the difference:

```ruby
module SuperDumbCrypto
  KEY = "password123"
end

class SuperDumbCrypto::Encrypt
  def initialize (key=KEY) # raises NameError
    ...
  end
end
```

This time a namespace and a lexical scope are created with the module definition, but immediately after creating the KEY constant both are closed. The class is defined in the correct namespace, but it doesn't share the same lexical scope as the KEY constant and so can't use it unqualified. This code raises a NameError exception because Ruby can't find the KEY constant in the lexical scope or through the inheritance hierarchy. The fix is simple—just qualify the constant:

```ruby
class SuperDumbCrypto::Encrypt
  def initialize (key=SuperDumbCrypto::KEY)
    ...
  end
end
```

It might seem a bit weird but that's how it works my friend. Even stranger still, now that the constant is fully qualified, it's actually found through the inheritance hierarchy and not the lexical scope. The SuperDumbCrypto constant can be considered a global constant, but as it turns out, Ruby doesn't actually have a global namespace. Instead all top-level constants are stored inside the Object class. Since almost everything in Ruby inherits from Object it can find top-level constants through the inheritance hierarchy. And that explains why Ruby looks in two different places: the current lexical scope and the inheritance hierarchy.

There's one last way you can get stuck when using namespaces. Consider this:

```ruby
module Cluster
  class Array
    def initialize (n)
      @disks = Array.new(n) {|i| "disk#{i}"}
      # Oops, wrong Array!  SystemStackError!
    end
  end
end
```

The code above defines a Cluster::Array class that needs to use the top-level Array class. The lookup rules for constants say that, in this context, an unqualified Array constant means Cluster::Array, which isn't what we want. The solution is to fully qualify the Array constant. Since it's a top-level constant and we know those are kept in the Object class, the fully qualified constant name would be Object::Array. This looks a bit strange, so Ruby allows us to abbreviate it as ::Array. The following code works as expected:

```ruby
module Cluster
  class Array
    def initialize (n)
      @disks = ::Array.new(n) {|i| "disk#{i}"}
    end
  end
end
```

While namespacing adds a bit of complexity—particularly for unqualified constants—the feature is well worth the cost. Any nontrivial Ruby project is bound to be using them, especially libraries that are packaged as a gem. Such libraries are expected to place all their constants under a namespace that matches the library name. Play nice with others by creating and using namespaces.

Things to Remember

+ Use modules to create namespaces by nesting definitions inside them.

+ Mirror your namespace structure and your directory structure.

+ Use "::" to fully qualify a top-level constant when its use would be ambiguous (e.g., ::Array).

Item 12: Understand the Different Flavors of Equality

Take a look at the following IRB session and ask yourself: Why does the equal? method return a different answer than the "==" operator?

```
irb> "foo" == "foo"
---> true

irb> "foo".equal?("foo")
---> false
```

As it turns out, there are actually four different ways to check if objects are equal to one another. Sometimes the various methods overlap and compare the same way, but as you can see above, that's not always the case. Depending on the comparison method and the objects involved, you can get surprising results. But they won't be for much longer.

It might seem like having four different ways to compare objects for equality is overkill. For most objects that's probably true since all four methods end up doing the same thing. But some give us several flavors of equality that often have subtle (and not so subtle) differences. For example, the various classes that represent numbers silently convert to one another when compared using the "==" operator:

```
irb> 1 == 1.0
---> true
```

Each time you define a class you inherit the four different equality testing methods. Understanding how they're expected to work is important if you want to override any of them. This is especially useful if you plan on implementing the full range of comparison operators as discussed in Item 13. We'll start with an easy one—the method that you're supposed to leave alone.

You may have been surprised in the example above when the equal? method didn't return the same result as the "==" operator. Obviously, they're testing two different things. I would venture so far as to say that equal? is a misnomer. Instead of comparing two objects based on their contents or values it's actually checking to see if the two objects are the exact same object. That is, if they both have the same object_id. (Internally, the implementation of equal? checks to see if the two objects are both pointers to the same chunk of memory.)

Even though the two strings above have identical contents, they're not the exact same object. They're two different objects that just happen to have the same characters. Each time Ruby evaluates a string literal it allocates a brand new String object, even if the same exact string already exists somewhere else in memory. Of course, that's what you want to happen. You wouldn't want to mutate a string only to find out that you've accidentally mutated every other string in your program that has the same contents. (If you're left wishing for copy-on-write strings you're not alone. But Ruby 2.1 has immutable string literals that share memory with other, identical strings. See Item 47 for details.)

An important point about the equal? method is that its behavior should be the same for all objects. That is, you shouldn't override this method and give it a different implementation. Several existing classes have come to rely on how this method works and changing it is sure to break things in strange ways. If you want to compare objects then using equal? probably isn't the method you want to use anyway. More often than not you'll be interested in the "==" operator.

When comparing objects, "==" does what you think it's going to do, and sometimes it will pleasantly surprise you. While each class is free to redefine "==", the agreed upon behavior is that it will return true if two objects represent the same *value*. That explains the earlier string comparison and the test between 1 and 1.0, which, by the way, are represented by two different classes, Fixnum and Float. This is probably more in line with what you would consider to be a comparison of equality.

If you don't write your own implementation of "==" you'll inherit the default implementation, which does same thing as the equal? method. This probably isn't very useful behavior. Obviously some objects should be considered equal even if they're not stored in the same memory location. Instead, you want the "==" operator to consider the contents of the objects being compared. Maybe it's as simple as comparing object attributes, record IDs, or delegating the comparison to another object. Either way, the "==" operator should be smarter than the equal? method. But resist the temptation to define "==" directly.

Item 13 explains how you can get "==" (and other operators) for free by defining the "<=>" operator and mixing in the Comparable module. If you're interested in defining ordering operators like ">" you should definitely consider the advice in that item.

The next method on our equality tour is ambiguously named and a bit obscure. Nevertheless, it's quite important. The eql? method is heavily used by the Hash class when comparing objects used as keys. You don't want to insert the same key in a hash more than once, and defining a reasonable eql? method only gets you halfway there. We'll look at the other half shortly.

By default eql? does the same comparison as equal?, and that's probably a bit stricter than what you want. If you define a class and use instances of that class as hash keys you'll be in for a surprise if you don't override the default implementation. Since the eql? method strictly compares objects based on their object_id you're likely to wind up with big hashes that don't behave the way you'd expect them to. For example, consider the Color class that follows.

```ruby
class Color
  def initialize (name)
    @name = name
  end
end
```

Look what happens if we create two instances of that class with the exact same values, then attempt to use them as hash keys:

```ruby
irb> a = Color.new("pink")
---> #<Color @name="pink">

irb> b = Color.new("pink")
---> #<Color @name="pink">

irb> {a => "like", b => "love"}
---> {#<Color @name="pink">=>"like", #<Color
@name="pink">=>"love"}
```

Without knowing about the eql? method you'd probably expect the final hash to only have one key, not two. To get the hash to collapse both keys into one we need to define an eql? method along with another important method—hash. When objects are used as keys the Hash class needs to decide where in the data structure the object will reside. It does this by calling the hash method on the key object. Two objects that represent the same key should always return the same value from the hash method. But it's also okay if dissimilar objects return the same hash value. That is, they don't have to be unique. When this happens it's called a collision, which is resolved by further comparing the key objects with eql?. Objects that have the same hash value and result in true when compared with eql? are considered the same key. So, if we want two similar Color objects to represent the same hash key we need to implement the hash method *and* the eql? method. For such a simple class we'll just manually delegate both to the @name attribute:

```ruby
class Color
  attr_reader(:name)

  def initialize (name)
    @name = name
  end

  def hash
    name.hash
  end
```

```
  def eql? (other)
    name.eql?(other.name)
  end
end
irb> a = Color.new("pink")
---> #<Color @name="pink">

irb> b = Color.new("pink")
---> #<Color @name="pink">

irb> {a => "like", b => "love"}
---> {#<Color @name="pink">=>"love"}
```

In most situations you probably want to implement the "<=>" operator as described in Item 13, then simply make eql? an alias for "==". So why even bother having an eql? method if it's just going to be an alias for the equality operator? That's a fair question. Let me answer it by reminding you of the type conversion done by the "==" operator in the numeric classes. Look again at how "==" and eql? differ for these classes:

```
irb> 3 == 3.0
---> true

irb> 3.eql?(3.0)
---> false

irb> {3 => "I'm Three!"}[3.0]
---> nil
```

It might be fine to consider 1 equal to 1.0 when using the "==" operator but not when using the eql? method, so that's why we have both. When defining your own classes you'll have to decide how objects compare with one another when used as hash keys. If you choose to implement a sloppy version of the "==" operator you'll need to define a stricter version of the eql? method. Otherwise, alias eql? to "==". I said it earlier but it's worth repeating: Remember that if you don't define eql? you'll pick up the default implementation, which uses the same logic as the equal? method.

Finally, let's take a look at an operator that you use all the time— maybe without even realizing it—the *case equality operator*. This operator is written with three equal signs ("==="), but it's most often used indirectly, through case expressions. See for yourself:

```
case command
when "start"          then start
when "stop", "quit" then stop
```

```
when /^cd\s+(.+)$/   then cd($1)
when Numeric          then timer(command)
else raise(InvalidCommandError, command)
end
```

There are two different ways to use a case expression. The one we're concerned with here is chosen by Ruby when you supply an expression to the case keyword (the command variable above). This flavor of case uses the "===" operator to compare the given expression to each of the when clauses. It's easier to see what's going on if you remove the syntactic sugar and reveal the underlying if expression:

```
if    "start" === command       then start
elsif "stop"  === command       then stop
elsif "quit"  === command       then stop
elsif /^cd\s+(.+)$/ === command then cd($1)
elsif Numeric === command       then timer(command)
else  raise(InvalidCommandError, command)
end
```

Notice that the expression given to the case keyword always ends up as the right operand to "===". That's important. In Ruby, the left operand becomes the receiver of the message and the right operand is the sole argument to the method call. It also means that in Ruby operators are not necessarily commutative because their behavior is decided by the left operand. Combining these two facts means you can rewrite the use of any operator as a normal method call:

```
irb> 1 + 2
---> 3
```

```
irb> 1.+(2)
---> 3
```

What does this have to do with the case equality operator? Well, for one thing it's important to know which object will wind up being the receiver. Knowing that the expression given to a when clause becomes the left operand to the "===" operator—and thus the receiver—tells you which implementation of the operator you're dealing with. Not surprisingly, Ruby core classes have useful variants of the case equality operator.

The default implementation of "===" is rather boring and passes its operands on to "==". This is the version you'll inherit in your classes. But things get interesting when you look at classes like Regexp. The Regexp class defines a "===" operator that returns true if its argument is a string that matches the receiver (the regular expression). You have to use the regular expression as the left operand; otherwise, you won't be using the "===" implementation from the Regexp class.

```
irb> /er/ === "Tyler" # Regexp#===
---> true
```

```
irb> "Tyler" === /er/ # String#===
---> false
```

Classes and modules also get into the act with class method versions of the "===" operator. They all share a common implementation that returns true if the right operand is an instance of the left operand. It's basically an operator version of the is_a? method with the receiver and argument reversed. This gives us the ability to use class and module names as arguments to the when clause. It's good to know how this works if you strip away the case syntax. Consider the similarities between is_a? and "===":

```
irb> [1,2,3].is_a?(Array)
---> true
```

```
irb> [1,2,3] === Array # Array#===
---> false
```

```
irb> Array === [1,2,3] # Array::===
---> true
```

It's unlikely that you'll need to define the "===" operator directly since the default implementation from Object is sufficient and can be found through inheritance. Still, if you want your objects or classes to have special behavior when used as an argument to the when clause in a case expression you'll know which operator to override. Just remember which operand becomes the receiver and which the argument.

Things to Remember

+ Never override the equal? method. It's expected to strictly compare objects and return true only if they're both pointers to the same object in memory (i.e., they both have the same object_id).

+ The Hash class uses the eql? method to compare objects used as keys during collisions. The default implementation probably doesn't do what you want. Follow the advice in Item 13 and then alias eql? to "==" and write a sensible hash method.

+ Use the "==" operator to test if two objects represent the same value. Some classes like those representing numbers have a sloppy equality operator that performs type conversion.

+ case expressions use the "===" operator to test each when clause. The left operand is the argument given to when and the right operand is the argument given to case.

Item 13: Implement Comparison via "<=>" and the Comparable Module

Item 12 discusses the four ways in which objects can be tested for equality. If you're also interested in sorting and comparing objects then you'll need to go one step further and define the remaining comparison operators. Unlike with the equality operators, classes don't inherit default implementations of the other comparison operators. Fortunately, Ruby gives us a shortcut, one we'll dig into shortly.

First, let's make this interesting and implement a class that has unusual ordering. As programmers we're so used to software version numbers that the strange notation doesn't seem to bother us much. But to the uninitiated it's unusual indeed. How do you compare "10.10.3" to "10.9.8"? The answer is obvious, but if we compared them using lexicographical ordering these version numbers would come out wrong. To get it right you need to consider each component separately. That's exactly what we'll do in our Version class.

To keep things reasonable let's work with version numbers that only have three parts (just like those above). The first part is the major version number, then the minor version number, and finally the patch level. We'll also only deal with well-formed version numbers so we can focus on comparing them. That makes it easy to parse a version string into its individual components.

```ruby
class Version
  attr_reader(:major, :minor, :patch)

  def initialize (version)
    @major, @minor, @patch =
      version.split('.').map(&:to_i)
  end
end
```

An important point that I want to repeat here is that classes don't automatically inherit comparison operators, but there's one exception. We'll see later that you only really need to define one comparison operator, namely "<=>". This particular operator is in fact inherited from Object, but the implementation we get for free is incomplete. See what happens if we try to sort an array of Version objects:

```ruby
irb> vs = %w(1.0.0  1.11.1  1.9.0).map {|v| Version.new(v)}
---> [ #<Version @major=1, @minor=0, @patch=0>,
       #<Version @major=1, @minor=11, @patch=1>,
       #<Version @major=1, @minor=9, @patch=0> ]
```

```
irb> vs.sort
ArgumentError: comparison of Version with Version failed
```

That's not very helpful. The default implementation of the "<=>" comparison operator is to blame here. It only considers whether two objects are equal to one another (using equal? and "===") and doesn't do the full range of testing our implementation needs to do. If the two objects being compared aren't equal to one another it returns nil, which signals to the sort method that the comparison is invalid. But that's okay. You can't expect much from a general-purpose implementation, so let's write our own.

Implementing the full range of comparison operators is done in two steps. The hardest part is writing a sensible "<=>" operator (informally referred to as the "spaceship" operator). Remember that in Ruby binary operators turn into method calls where the left operand is the receiver and the right operand is the method's first and only argument. When writing a comparison operator it's common practice to name the argument "other" since it will be the other object you're comparing the receiver to.

The "<=>" operator can stand in for the full range of comparison operators due to the flexibility of its return value. It can return one of four values:

- When it doesn't make sense to compare the receiver with the argument then the comparison operator should return nil. It's possible that the argument is an instance of another class or even nil. For some classes it might be useful to convert the argument to the correct type before doing the comparison, but more often it's best to return nil if the receiver and argument are not instances of the same class. That's what we'll do with the Version class.

- If the receiver is less than the argument, return -1. In other words, if comparing the left and right operands with "<" should return true then you want "<=>" to return negative one.

- If the receiver is greater than the argument, return 1. This comparison is for the ">" operator. If comparing the left and right operands with ">" should return true then make sure "<=>" returns positive one.

- If the receiver is equal to the argument, return 0. The "==" operator will return true only when "<=>" returns zero.

We want the comparison operator for the Version class to work the way it does in the numeric classes. As a matter of fact, we'll be able to implement our version in terms of the numeric one. As you can see, it follows the rules from above:

```
irb> 9 <=> "9"
---> nil

irb> 9 <=> 10
---> -1

irb> 10 <=> 9
---> 1

irb> 10 <=> 10
---> 0
```

When writing the "<=>" operator it's often possible to delegate the comparison to an object's instance variables. The three variables in the Version class are all instances of Fixnum, which has a working implementation of the "<=>" operator. This greatly simplifies our work. To compare version numbers we need to consider the instance variables in the receiver (left operand) and those from the argument (right operand) in order from major number to patch level. We can stop comparing as soon as one of the variables from the receiver doesn't equal the corresponding variable from the argument. In other words, if the two versions we're comparing have different major numbers we don't need to compare the minor numbers or patch levels to know which is greater than the other. But if both major numbers are the same, we'll need to repeat the comparison with the minor numbers and so on to the patch levels. When all components are equal to one another our comparison operator should return 0 to indicate the equality of both version objects. Otherwise, we just need to return the result of using "<=>" for the first pair of variables that don't match. Consider the Version implementation of the comparison operator:

```
def <=> (other)
  return nil unless other.is_a?(Version)

  [ major <=> other.major,
    minor <=> other.minor,
    patch <=> other.patch,
  ].detect {|n| !n.zero?} || 0
end
```

Each component is compared separately and the results are stored in an array. All we need to do then is find the first nonzero element in the array (the first pair of components that isn't equal). If all components are equal to one another then detect will return nil, in which case the method will return 0. Now we can sort an array of Version objects.

```
irb> vs = %w(1.0.0  1.11.1  1.9.0).map {|v| Version.new(v)}
---> [ #<Version @major=1, @minor=0, @patch=0>,
       #<Version @major=1, @minor=11, @patch=1>,
       #<Version @major=1, @minor=9, @patch=0> ]

irb> vs.sort
---> [ #<Version @major=1, @minor=0, @patch=0>,
       #<Version @major=1, @minor=9, @patch=0>,
       #<Version @major=1, @minor=11, @patch=1> ]
```

There's one more piece of code we'll need to add in order for Version objects to be fully comparable. Beyond just sorting, we want to be able to use operators such as ">" and ">=" with these objects. As a matter of fact, there are actually five other operators that make up the full set of ordering operators: "<", "<=", "==", ">", and ">=". You'll be happy to hear that we don't have to implement them by hand. Instead, all we need to do is include the Comparable module.

```
class Version
  include(Comparable)
  ...
end
```

That's it. Now we can use all of the ordering operators and even one additional helper method:

```
irb> a = Version.new('2.1.1')
---> #<Version @major=2, @minor=1, @patch=1>

irb> b = Version.new('2.10.3')
---> #<Version @major=2, @minor=10, @patch=3>

irb> [a > b, a >= b, a < b, a <= b, a == b]
---> [false, false, true, true, false]

irb> Version.new('2.8.0').between?(a, b)
---> true
```

There are a few final considerations when using the Comparable module. First, for some classes you might want to implement your own copy of the "==" operator so it's fuzzier than the one from Comparable. A good example was presented in Item 12, which showed that the numeric classes perform type conversions before making comparisons. If you want this to happen you'll have to write your own equality operator or change the conditions that cause "<=>" to return 0. The option you choose depends on how you want the other comparison operators to be affected.

If you want ">=", "<=", and "==" to return consistent answers you should change the way "<=>" calculates equality. If they don't need to be consistent with one another you can simply override "==" and make it less strict than the other comparison operators. But for most classes, you'll probably want to make all the operators consistent with one another.

Finally, if you want instances of your class to be usable as hash keys you'll need to do two more things. First, the eql? method should become an alias for "==". The default implementation of eql? does the same thing as equal?, which doesn't make sense if you have a "<=>" operator defined for your class. The alias will make the Hash class use the "==" operator defined by the Comparable module.

You'll also need to define a hash method that returns a Fixnum. To get the best performance from the Hash class you should ensure that different objects return different hash values. The following is a simple example implementation for the Version class. (Writing an optimized version of hash is outside the scope of this book.)

```ruby
class Version
    ...
    alias_method(:eql?, :==)

    def hash
        [major, minor, patch].hash
    end
end
```

Things to Remember

+ Implement object ordering by defining a "<=>" operator and including the Comparable module.

+ The "<=>" operator should return nil if the left operand can't be compared with the right.

+ If you implement "<=>" for a class you should consider aliasing eql? to "==", especially if you want instances to be usable as hash keys, in which case you should also override the hash method.

Item 14: Share Private State through Protected Methods

One of the major tenets of OOP is encapsulation, the idea that an object's internal implementation will be just that, internal and hidden from the outside. This allows us to build a firewall. On one side we have the public interface that we advertise for others to use. Hidden on the other side is the private implementation that we're free to change without fear of breaking anything external to the class. In Ruby this barrier is more theoretical than concrete, but it's there nonetheless.

Take instance variables as an example—they're private by default. Without resorting to any backdoor metaprogramming they're only accessible from within instance methods. If you want to expose them to the outside world you need to define so-called accessor methods. This is good news. You can safely store internal state in instance variables without worrying that it will accidentally become part of the public interface. Most of the time this is all fine and good, but there's one situation where this sort of encapsulation gets in the way. Sometimes one object needs to access the internal state of another. Consider this:

```ruby
class Widget
  def overlapping? (other)
    x1, y1 = @screen_x, @screen_y
    x2, y2 = other.instance_eval {[@screen_x, @screen_y]}
    ...
  end
end
```

The Widget#overlapping? method checks to see if the receiver and another object overlap one another on the screen. The public interface for the Widget class doesn't expose these screen coordinates; they're an internal implementation detail. It would seem that our only alternative is to break the wall of encapsulation using some metaprogramming. But this approach has its drawbacks.

Usually, when designing classes with internal state, it's a good idea to reduce the amount of code that accesses the state directly to the smallest number of methods possible. This makes it easier to test and reduces the amount of breakage when things change. Hiding state behind private methods also facilitates optimizations such as memoization (see Item 48). It's better for maintainability if the Widget class keeps the screen coordinates private, even to the overlapping? method. You might be tempted to write a private method to act as a gateway for the screen coordinates, but that won't work in this situation.

Private methods behave differently in Ruby than they do in other OOP languages. Ruby only places one restriction on private methods—they can't be called with an explicit receiver. It doesn't matter where you are in the inheritance hierarchy. As long as you don't use a receiver you can call private methods defined in superclasses. But what you can't do is call private methods on another object, even when the caller and receiver have the same class. If you make the screen coordinates accessible through a private method you still won't be able to use them in the overlapping? method. Thankfully Ruby has an answer to this: protected methods.

Where private methods can't be used with a receiver, protected methods can. But there's just one catch, and it's a slightly complicated one. The method being invoked on the receiver must also be in the inheritance hierarchy of the caller. As long as both the caller and receiver both share the same instance method through inheritance then the caller can invoke that method on the receiver. The caller and receiver don't necessarily have to be instances of the same class, but they both have to share the superclass where the method is defined.

For the Widget class, we can define a method that exposes the private screen coordinates without making them part of the public interface. By declaring this method as protected we maintain encapsulation while allowing the overlapping? method to access both its own coordinates and those of the other widget. No metaprogramming black magic required!

```ruby
class Widget
  def overlapping? (other)
    x1, y1 = screen_coordinates
    x2, y2 = other.screen_coordinates
    ...
  end

  protected

  def screen_coordinates
    [@screen_x, @screen_y]
  end
end
```

This is exactly what protected methods were designed to do—share private information between related classes.

Things to Remember

✦ Share private state through protected methods.

✦ Protected methods can only be called with an explicit receiver from objects of the same class or when they inherit the protected methods from a common superclass.

Item 15: Prefer Class Instance Variables to Class Variables

Ruby has two types of "at" variables: instance variables and class variables. Every object in a running Ruby application has its own private set of instance variables, you know, the ones whose names begin with "@". Setting an instance variable in one object doesn't affect variables in another. (But mutating a variable is a different story; two objects sharing a reference to a third can certainly affect one another. See Item 16 for more information.)

Class variables (those which begin with "@@") are handled differently. Instead of being associated with a single object, they're attached to a class and visible to all instances of that class. Setting a class variable in one object is immediately visible to another. Of course, this isn't surprising, most object-oriented languages have these class-wide shared variables. But what might be surprising is how class variables and inheritance interact.

A common use for class variables—but certainly not the only use— is implementing the singleton pattern (not to be confused with Ruby singleton classes). Sometimes in larger applications you only want a single instance of a particular class, and you want all of the code to access the same instance. Take a configuration class, for example. You'd like to parse your configuration file once and then share it with the entire application, but without having to pass it around as an argument to every method that might need it. Basically, the singleton pattern is used for objects that are glorified global variables.

Setting aside concurrency for a moment, let's write a class that implements the singleton pattern and from which we can derive other classes:

```ruby
class Singleton
  private_class_method(:new, :dup, :clone)

  def self.instance
    @@single ||= new
  end
end
```

By their very definition singleton classes shouldn't have more than one instance, so it's pretty typical to make the new method private. This prevents anyone from creating a new object from the outside. We do the same thing with dup and clone to ensure copies of the one true instance can't be made. The only way to access this official object is through the instance class method. Its job is to make sure new is only called once and it does this by storing the singleton object in a class variable named @@single. If that variable is nil the instance method will call new and assign the result to @@single. Otherwise, it simply returns the value of @@single. Let's create two classes that inherit from the Singleton class so that they can use the same logic:

```
class Configuration < Singleton
  ...
end

class Database < Singleton
  ...
end
```

So far so good. An application using these classes now has a way to access a single configuration object and a single database connection from anywhere in the code. But I wouldn't be writing this if there wasn't a problem, so let's see what happens when we actually try to use these classes:

```
irb> Configuration.instance
---> #<Configuration>

irb> Database.instance
---> #<Configuration>
```

Oops. What happened? Obviously, both classes share the same class variable. When Configuration::instance is called the @@single variable is nil and so new is called and the resulting object is cached. When Database::instance is called @@single already has a value (the configuration object) and that's returned instead of calling new. The fix is easy but requires a little explanation.

Class variables in a superclass are shared between it and all of its subclasses. To make things a little messier, any instance of one of these classes can access the shared class variables and modify them. Instance methods and class methods all share the same class variables, making them as undesirable as global variables. So instances should stick to working with instance variables. And therein lies the solution. Classes are objects, so they have instance variables too. Every class is a unique object and has its own private set of instance variables that can only be accessed from its class methods. Changing the @@single variable from a class variable to a *class instance variable* fixes the problem:

```
def self.instance
  @single ||= new
end

irb> Configuration.instance
---> #<Configuration>

irb> Database.instance
---> #<Database>
```

If you haven't seen instance variables inside a class method before it can be a bit strange. It's also easy to confuse them with instance variables from one of their objects. But they do in fact belong to the class itself. This is easier to understand if you remember that class methods are really an illusion. Because classes are objects, what we call "class methods" are actually instance methods for the class object. Class methods exist in name only.

Besides breaking the sharing relationship between a class and its subclasses, class instance variables also provide more encapsulation. While class variables ("@@") can be accessed and modified directly from any instance or class method, class instance variables ("@") are only accessible at the class definition level or from inside class methods. So, instances of the class and other external code can only access these variables if you provide class methods for that purpose (e.g., Singleton::instance). You get to protect them just like any other instance variable, giving access to them as necessary.

Oh, by the way, earlier I asked that we set aside any issues relating to concurrency. That's because class variables and class instance variables have the same problems that global variables do. If your application has multiple threads of control then altering any of these variables without using a mutex isn't safe. Thankfully, the Singleton module, which is part of the Ruby standard library, correctly implements the singleton pattern in a thread-safe way. Using it is simple:

```
require('singleton')

class Configuration
  include(Singleton)
end
```

Things to Remember

+ Prefer class instance variables to class variables.

+ Classes are objects and so have their own private set of instance variables.

3

Collections

It's tempting to think of Ruby's collection classes as containers. If you squint and focus on the two rock stars of the core library, Array and Hash, this is certainly true. But what about the often-used Range class? Is it a container? Does having an each method and including the Enumerable module make a class a *container*?

Alright...I might have stretched that a bit far. You already know that Ruby has several classes that are clearly not containers but use Enumerable. That's why we throw around the term "collection," which is sometimes synonymous with "container," but obviously not always. The first classes you probably played around with while learning Ruby are either Array or Hash. That's because they're really simple to use and easy to understand, but no less powerful than their counterparts in other languages. In this chapter I'll spend a little bit of time with these classes, but only long enough to show off some of the features you might have missed. However, mostly I'll focus on staying out of trouble when using the collection classes and some of the Ruby features that tend to bite beginner and intermediate Ruby programmers.

Speaking of things that might trip you up, newcomers often shy away from the confusing reduce method (also known as inject). I will shed some light on that misunderstood Enumerable method and hopefully give you a new trick for your toolbox along the way. You'll be folding collections like the pros, which, believe it or not, is actually pretty useful. How useful? How about incrementally converting an array into a hash without needing any temporary variables? You know, fun stuff.

Item 16: Duplicate Collections Passed as Arguments before Mutating Them

As you know, the collection classes in Ruby hold a group of objects, but what does that really entail? When you insert an object into an array, what are you actually inserting? A copy of the object? The original? The answer actually depends on the class of the object.

Most objects are passed around as references and not as actual values. When these types of objects are inserted into a container the collection class is actually storing a reference to the object and not the object itself. (The notable exception to this rule is the Fixnum class whose objects are always passed by value and not by reference.)

The same is true when objects are passed as method arguments. The method will receive a reference to the object and not a new copy. This is great for efficiency but has a startling implication. The act of modifying an object is observable by any code that holds a reference to it. Mutating an element of an array affects the original object, which may still be available outside of the array. Similarly, when a method alters one of its arguments, those changes are visible outside of the method. Sometimes that's the entire point of the method and its author was kind enough to suffix the method name with "!". But most of the time you really don't want your objects to be mutated behind your back.

Collections (such as arrays and hashes) tend to be modified a lot during their lifetime. A common mistake among new Ruby programmers is to mutate a collection that was passed as an argument to a method, often without realizing that the original collection will also be modified. Throw in a little indirection and it's easy to see how something like this can happen.

As an example, consider the following class, which represents a radio tuner. The class supports the notion of station presets—commonly found in car stereos—by which a user can jump to a favorite frequency by pressing a single button. When a Tuner object is initialized it's given an array of preset stations, which it then sanitizes to ensure all of the frequencies are valid.

```ruby
class Tuner
  def initialize (presets)
    @presets = presets
    clean
  end

  private

  def clean
    # Valid frequencies end in odd digits.
    @presets.delete_if {|f| f[-1].to_i.even?}
  end
end
```

```
irb> presets = %w(90.1 106.2 88.5)
---> ["90.1", "106.2", "88.5"]

irb> tuner = Tuner.new(presets)
---> #<Tuner @presets=["90.1", "88.5"]>

irb> presets
---> ["90.1", "88.5"]
```

If you are using the Tuner class and expect the array passed to new to remain unchanged, well, you'll be in for a surprise. Mutating arguments that are given to a method is an easy mistake to make, especially when the changes are made by nested method calls like in the Tuner class. It's even more troublesome when the internal state of one object is passed as an argument to another and then subsequently modified. These types of bugs often go unnoticed and untested due to complex interactions between objects.

It might seem like the best course of action would be to simply avoid mutating method arguments in the first place. For some classes this might actually be the easiest approach. The Tuner class, for example, could use Array#reject instead of Array#delete_if. This would work because reject returns a *new* array (with possibly fewer elements than the original) instead of mutating the receiver. Updating Tuner to use this strategy is fairly trivial.

```
class Tuner
  def initialize (presets)
    @presets = clean(presets)
  end

  private

  def clean (presets)
    presets.reject {|f| f[-1].to_i.even?}
  end
end
```

This time, the array given to Tuner::new is not the same array that is kept in @presets. Unfortunately, things aren't always this simple. What if you don't need to mutate the collection upfront, during initialization, but later on in other instance methods? If you mistakenly take an argument given to initialize and stash it away in an instance variable you'll still run into trouble if you later modify it. What you really want in these situations is a copy of the collection instead of a reference to the original. Then you're free to mutate it to your heart's content. But stay with me for a few more moments so you're not surprised by how object copying works.

Ruby comes with two methods for creating copies of objects: dup and clone. Both create new objects based on the receiver, but clone preserves two additional features of the original object that dup does not. First, clone respects the frozen state of the receiver. If the original object is frozen then the copy will also be frozen. This is different than dup, which never returns a frozen object. Second, if the receiver has singleton methods clone will also duplicate the singleton class. Because dup doesn't do this, the original object and the copy may not respond to the same messages. Most of the time you'll want to use dup instead of clone, especially when you plan on mutating the resulting object. Frozen objects cannot be modified or unfrozen, so clone could potentially return an immutable object. Since we want to mutate the new object, dup is the way to go. Now we can resurrect the first Tuner implementation and fix it using dup:

```ruby
class Tuner
  def initialize (presets)
    @presets = presets.dup
    clean # Modifies the duplicate.
  end
  ...
end
```

It's a common pattern to duplicate collection objects given as method arguments. But watch out—it comes with a warning label. You need to be aware that dup and clone return shallow copies. For collection classes like Array this means the container is duplicated but the elements aren't. You can add and remove elements without affecting the original collection, but the same can't be said of the elements themselves. The original collection and the copy both reference the same element objects. Modifying an element will be visible in both collections and to the outside world.

```ruby
irb> a = ["Polar"]

irb> b = a.dup << "Bear"
---> ["Polar", "Bear"]

irb> b.each {|x| x.sub!('lar', 'oh')}
---> ["Pooh", "Bear"]

irb> a
---> ["Pooh"]
```

When writing your own class you can override the initialize_copy method to control the depth of the duplication process. But if you need deep copies of the existing collection classes, you'll have to roll your own. Thankfully, there's a quick solution that works most of the time. You can use the Marshal class to serialize and then deserialize the collection and its elements:

```
irb> a = ["Monkey", "Brains"]

irb> b = Marshal.load(Marshal.dump(a))

irb> b.each(&:upcase!); b.first
---> "MONKEY"

irb> a.last
---> "Brains"
```

The Marshal trick comes with its fair share of limitations. Besides the time it takes to serialize and deserialize an object, you also have to consider the amount of memory needed. The duplicated object will, of course, occupy its own memory space, but so will the serialized byte stream created by Marshal::dump. Dumping and loading large objects can certainly turn your program into a memory hog.

A potentially even bigger problem is that not all objects can be serialized with Marshal. Objects that contain closures or those with singleton methods cannot be serialized. Some of the core Ruby classes also don't work with Marshal. These include the IO and File classes, for example. In all these cases a TypeError exception will be raised from Marshal::dump.

This might seem like a lot of trouble to go through (and you're right), but you'll rarely need to turn to Marshal to create deep copies of objects. Most often, just duplicating the container is enough to keep the surprise factor low. But knowing these limitations will keep you out of trouble when you do need deep copies.

Things to Remember

+ Method arguments in Ruby are passed as references, not values. Notable exceptions to this rule are Fixnum objects.

+ Duplicate collections passed as arguments before mutating them.

+ The dup and clone methods only create shallow copies.

+ For most objects, Marshal can be used to create deep copies when needed.

Item 17: Use the Array Method to Convert nil and Scalar Objects into Arrays

In statically typed languages like C++ you can have several implementations of a single method just so long as they differ in their arguments. While this isn't something we can do directly in Ruby, it's often emulated using duck typing. That is, we write a single method that accepts any kind of object as an argument, as long as that argument responds to an expected set of messages. In other words, Ruby programmers prefer to work with interfaces over types. Unfortunately, that's not always possible.

We often need to be able to handle situations where a variable isn't what we expected it to be. This tends to happen a lot with arrays. The implementation of a method might expect an array as an argument but the caller wants to pass in a single object. Sometimes that single object is nil when it really should be an empty array. The same thing can happen with the return value of a method. It might return a single object, an array, or even nil. If you're like me you'd rather handle all of these situations uniformly.

Consider for a moment a class used for ordering pizza:

```
class Pizza
  def initialize (toppings)
    toppings.each do |topping|
     add_and_price_topping(topping)
    end
  end

  ...
end
```

The initialize method expects an array of toppings but we'd like to be able to pass in a single topping, or possibly nil when there are no toppings. You might be tempted to reach for variable-length argument lists by changing the argument to *toppings, thus collapsing all arguments into a single array. While this allows us to pass in a single topping, an array of toppings can no longer be given directly without using "*" to explode the array as it's passed to initialize. So all we've done is trade one problem for another. A better solution is to convert the incoming argument into an array so we know for sure what we're working with.

Tucked away in the Kernel module is a method with an unusual name, Array. That's right, a method name that starts with an uppercase letter. While Ruby is nearly draconian when it comes to the names of constants, it's much less restrictive with method names. This is also one of those times where parentheses really help clarify what's going on because it's easy to confuse the Array class and the Array method. So, what does this method do? Unsurprisingly, it converts its argument to an array. The great thing about this method is how it converts different objects into arrays. Most objects are converted into an array that contains one element. It's also smart enough to turn nil values into empty arrays. See for yourself:

```
irb> Array('Betelgeuse')
---> ["Betelgeuse"]
```

```
irb> Array(nil)
---> []

irb> Array(['Nadroj', 'Retep'])
---> ["Nadroj", "Retep"]
```

As you can see from the last example, if the argument is already an array then the Array method simply passes it through as its return value. The way other objects are converted is pretty straightforward as well. If the argument to Array responds to either the to_ary or to_a message then that method is called. If neither method can be called on the argument then Array wraps the argument in a new array and returns this single-element array. Most of the time this works exactly as you'd expect, but look what happens when you pass the Array method a hash:

```
irb> h = {pepperoni: 20, jalapenos: 2}

irb> Array(h)
---> [[:pepperoni, 20], [:jalapenos, 2]]
```

Each key-value pair is converted into a two-element array that Hash#to_a then nests into another array. This might not seem very useful but it does completely represent the source hash, and the resulting array can be used to reconstruct the original hash using the Hash::[] method. While Hash#to_a and Hash::[] might be great for converting a hash to and from an array, they unfortunately present a problem with our use of the Array method. That is, they're incompatible with this technique. If you want to write a method that can accept either an array of hashes or a single hash you'll have to resort to something other than using the Array method. But if you're dealing with an array of hashes, you might want to consider the advice in Item 10.

Back to pizza toppings, we can now simplify the Pizza initialization interface using the Array method trick:

```
class Pizza
  def initialize (toppings)
   Array(toppings).each do |topping|
     add_and_price_topping(topping)
   end
  end

  ...
end
```

With a really small change to the initialize method it can now take an array of toppings, a single topping, or even no toppings at all (nil or []). Potentially more important, the change makes the code more robust in the presence of a `nil` value that could accidentally wind up as the argument to `initialize`. That's a nice win all by itself.

Things to Remember

+ Use the `Array` method to convert `nil` and scalar objects into arrays.

+ Don't pass a `Hash` to the `Array` method; it will get converted into a set of nested arrays.

Item 18: Consider `Set` for Efficient Element Inclusion Checking

No doubt you're familiar with and most likely very comfortable using the core collection classes. Both `Array` and `Hash` are integral to every-day Ruby programming, and let's not forget `Range`. All three classes are woven into the language with dedicated syntax for creating objects from literals. Being part of the core library also means you don't have to do anything special before using them, that is, no library to load or file to require. These classes are so predominant in Ruby programs that sometimes they're used even when a more appropriate class for the task at hand is available.

Part of the problem might be that Ruby ships with two different librar-ies. The core library is preloaded in every program and includes most of the famous collection classes you've grown to love. Then there's the standard library. It's quite a bit bigger than the core library, so it's not loaded automatically. Before you can use any class from the standard library you have to require the correct file. This one extra step seems to make a big difference when it comes to discovering the wealth of classes and modules in the standard library.

Take the `Set` class, for example. It's a very useful collection class but since it's part of the standard library you have to require a file before using it. Based on its name alone you probably already have a good idea of what it does. It's a lot like its mathematical cousin, a collec-tion of unordered unique elements with operations such as union, intersection, and subset/superset testing. While there are definitely times when it's handy to have a mathematical set class easily avail-able, I want to talk about one specific feature of `Set`, element inclusion testing.

As a way to play with sets, let's explore a watered down version of a class that provides role-based authorization. Typically, a role rep-resents a grouping of permissions. Before a user can perform an action you iterate through all roles associated with the user to see if any of them allow the action. Consider this very simple implementation, which stores the collection of permissions in an array:

```ruby
class Role
  def initialize (name, permissions)
    @name, @permissions = name, permissions
  end

  def can? (permission)
    @permissions.include?(permission)
  end
end
```

There are two parts to this implementation. The Role class expects to be given an array of permissions and in return it provides a can? method that can be used to test if the role supports a specific permission. The implementation is grossly oversimplified, but stay with me for just a bit.

In the initialize method this array of permissions is stashed away in the @permissions instance variable without having to convert it or manipulate it in any way. This makes it easy to write the can? method since we just need to see if a permission is an element of the array using the include? method. You might have noticed that the array is only being used for its ability to be a container of elements. The @permissions variable could really be any container that supports the include? method. As a matter of fact, out of all the collection classes, Array has the worst-performing include? method with a time complexity of $O(n)$. As the number of permissions in the array grows so does the time needed to check if an element is contained within it. This also means that each time the can? method is called to check a permission, and that permission isn't in the @permissions array, the entire array needs to be consulted before we can return false. But we can do better than that, much better.

After an array gets big enough that include? becomes a real performance concern, most Ruby programmers turn to Hash. While a hash requires more memory for its internal data structure, accessing elements can be done in roughly $O(\log n)$. That's a big improvement over Array. The only (slightly) annoying thing about using a hash in the Role class is its construction. Hashes store keys *and* values, but we don't have any values to store, we just have a list of permissions. When using a hash this way, it's common practice to use true as the hash value so that all elements in the hash reference the same immutable global variable. Here's an updated Role class that uses Hash instead of Array:

```ruby
class Role
  def initialize (name, permissions)
```

```
    @name = name
    @permissions = Hash[permissions.map {|p| [p, true]}]
  end

  def can? (permission)
    @permissions.include?(permission)
  end
end
```

The only change is in the `initialize` method where we need to convert the incoming array into a hash. But there are two trade-offs you need to know. First, since `Hash` only stores unique keys, any duplicates in the array will be lost when converted into a hash. In this case, the loss is completely reasonable since duplicate permissions in a role are nonsensical. If you want to preserve duplicates then this technique isn't appropriate.

Second, in order to convert the array into a hash we need to map over the entire array and construct an even bigger array that then gets fed to `Hash::[]`. This shifts the performance burden from the `can?` method to the `initialize` method with the assumption that `can?` is called more often than `initialize`. If `Role` objects are created and destroyed with the `can?` method only ever being called a small number of times, we're probably not saving any time by trying to optimize with `Hash`. If, on the other hand, the hash was incrementally built over time instead of all at once in `initialize`, this would still be a good technique. (A good way to incrementally build a hash like this is by using the `reduce` method, which is discussed in Item 19.)

Converting the array of permissions into a hash is pretty simple, although a bit ugly with all those braces. And just as with the `Array` version before it, we're not really using any of the unique features `Hash` provides. That is, we're only using it to test for element inclusion. Wouldn't it be nice to abstract away the hash construction code in `initialize` and clean this code up a bit? I sure think so, and that's where `Set` comes in.

```
require('set')

class Role
  def initialize (name, permissions)
    @name, @permissions = name, Set.new(permissions)
  end

  def can? (permission)
    @permissions.include?(permission)
  end
end
```

This version of the `Role` class is very similar to the first version, which used the `Array` class. This is mostly due to the fact that `Set` objects can be constructed from any collection object or enumerator. Essentially, Set::new is doing the conversion for us (and incrementally too). On the plus side, the Set version performs nearly as good as the Hash version. Internally, the Set class stores its elements in a Hash. This means that the trade-offs for using Hash also apply when using Set. Namely, that duplicate elements are lost and the original array needs to be converted into a hash. There's also a requirement that objects stored in the set are well-behaved hash keys, which is the same requirement the previous version of the Role class had, but this time it's implicit.

Since the array given to Set::new must be converted into a hash it might not be convincing that using Set in this case is worthwhile. Again, if the number of calls to can? doesn't exceed the number of calls to initialize it's probably not worth the conversion. If you don't need to perform a conversion but need to test for element inclusion often then Set can be a real win for performance and ease of use. To illustrate this let's go back to the example code from Item 10.

As a brief reminder, the example class processed weather data from a CSV file. Each row in the CSV file represents a single month of data and is stored in a Reading struct, which is then inserted into an array. To make things more interesting, let's say that the CSV file might contain duplicate rows. When encountering a duplicate we'd like to keep the most recently read row, discarding the previous value. But guess what? We only need to make two simple changes to the existing code. The Reading class needs to be changed so its objects can be used as hash keys and the AnnualWeather#initialize method needs to be changed to use Set instead of Array. See for yourself:

```ruby
require('set')
require('csv')

class AnnualWeather
  Reading = Struct.new(:date, :high, :low) do
    def eql? (other) date.eql?(other.date); end
    def hash; date.hash; end
  end

  def initialize (file_name)
    @readings = Set.new

    CSV.foreach(file_name, headers: true) do |row|
      @readings << Reading.new(Date.parse(row[2]),
                               row[10].to_f,
                               row[11].to_f)
    end
  end
end
```

Because Set includes Enumerable and provides an interface similar to that of Array nothing else needs to change. This version automatically ensures that there are no duplicate records in the collection, and the duplicate detection is fast. Since the Reading objects are ultimately stored in a hash and their uniqueness is based on their date, the eql? and hash methods just delegate to the date attribute. That's not a lot of code for a big win. But there is a downside.

Arrays are ordered containers. In the version of AnnualWeather that used an array, the elements were in the same order in the array that they were read from the CSV file. That's not necessarily the case with Set, which is an unordered container. The array version also allowed random access to any element given its index. There's no way to access individual elements in a Set by indexing into it. To do that, you'd first have to convert it into an array. (Technically speaking, since Set actually uses a hash under the covers the elements should be accessible in the order in which they were inserted. That said, the documentation for Set clearly states that the container is unordered. In other words, the fact that the elements are actually ordered is an implementation detail that is subject to change. If you truly need ordered sets you might want to consider the SortedSet class, which is also part of the standard library.)

If you don't need the elements to be in any specific order, don't need random access to individual elements, and you need efficient checking for element inclusion, Set is the class for you. Just remember to require the "set" file before using it.

Things to Remember

✦ Consider Set for efficient element inclusion checking.

✦ Objects inserted into a Set must also be usable as hash keys.

✦ Require the "set" file before using Set.

Item 19: Know How to Fold Collections with reduce

Classes that include the Enumerable module gain a wealth of instance methods for filtering, traversing, and transforming collections of objects. Among them are the ever-popular map and select, powerful methods at the core of nearly all Ruby programs. Collection classes such as Array and Hash are so integral to writing Ruby programs that if you're not familiar with the methods defined in Enumerable you're probably writing more code than you ought to and really missing out.

But right now, I want to talk about one particular method in Enumerable, one method to rule them all. One you should definitely understand and be comfortable with. Yes, I'm talking about reduce, also known as inject. (I like neither name but if I have to pick one, I'll go with reduce. Before Ruby 1.9 reduce wasn't an option so you're likely to see inject more often.)

What does reduce do and what's so special about it? In functional programming terms, it's a folding function that transforms one data structure into another. One of the things that makes it so powerful yet frustratingly confusing is how general it is. Programmers new to Ruby who don't have a background in functional programming often have a hard time with the reduce method. But don't worry—we're going to explore several sides to reduce and by the end of this item you'll have a new power tool at your disposal.

Let's start by taking a bird's eye view of folding. When working with folding functions such as reduce you need to understand three main components:

- An enumerable object, which is the receiver of the reduce message. This is the source collection that you want to transform in some way. Its class must obviously include Enumerable; otherwise, you wouldn't be able to call reduce on it.

- A block, which is invoked once for each element in the source collection, similar to how the each method invokes its block. But unlike with each, the block given to reduce must produce a return value. The return value represents the final data structure with the current element *folded* into it. We'll work through some examples that make this more concrete in a bit.

- An object that is the starting value for the destination data structure, known as the accumulator. Each invocation of the block accepts the current accumulator value and returns a new accumulator value. After all elements have been folded into the accumulator, its final value becomes the return value from reduce.

The obligatory example when demonstrating reduce is a method that sums an array of numbers. In this case, you can think of reduce as folding a collection of numbers into a single number. The starting value (accumulator) should be zero because if the array is empty— and therefore the block is never invoked—it's the only valid result. Consider the following implementation of sum:

```
def sum (enum)
  enum.reduce(0) do |accumulator, element|
    accumulator + element
  end
end
```

The argument given to reduce is the starting value for the accumulator. It's also the first argument that is yielded to the block. The purpose of the block is to create and return a new accumulator that is then fed into the next iteration of the block. The accumulator returned from the last iteration becomes the return value for reduce. If the source collection is empty then the block is never executed and reduce simply returns the initial accumulator value.

Notice that the block doesn't make any assignments. It's important to realize that mutating the accumulator won't always have the desired effect. That's because after each iteration reduce throws away the previous accumulator and keeps the return value of the block as the new accumulator. If you mutate the accumulator and return nil from the block then the accumulator for the next iteration will be nil, which is probably not what you wanted.

Take another look at the block used in the sum method. For each iteration the block is yielded the current accumulator value along with the current element, which are then added together. This sum then becomes the return value for the block and hence the accumulator for the next iteration. The process repeats until all elements have been passed to the block. The final accumulator value is then returned from reduce.

There's a dangerous shortcut offered by reduce—it lets you omit the starting value for the accumulator. When you do this reduce will use the first element in the source collection as the accumulator and start the iteration cycle on the second element. The reason this is dangerous is that if the source collection is empty then reduce will return nil instead of something sensible. Most uses of reduce should not return nil since it's so easy to have it return the starting value. So I recommend that you always use a starting value for the accumulator.

Another shortcut that is sometimes handy deals with the block itself. Instead of giving reduce a block you can give it a symbol. On each iteration reduce will send a message to the accumulator using the symbol as the message name, passing the current element as an argument. This allows us to express sum more concisely:

```ruby
def sum (enum)
  enum.reduce(0, :+)
end
```

If you're used to generating blocks on the fly with the "&" operator it might look weird to pass a bare symbol to reduce. Don't worry—in this case, &:+ will also work. Both basically do the same thing, but the version with "&" is more familiar since that's what's used with methods like map and each.

Personally, I think that using sum as an example is quite boring, so let's do something more interesting and use reduce to transform an array into a hash. Back in Item 18 we converted an array into a hash by essentially duplicating the array and feeding it into Hash::[]. The elements of the array became the keys and true was used for the values. Here's what it looked like:

```
Hash[array.map {|x| [x, true]}]
```

Let's save some space and build the hash incrementally. Guess which method is prefect for this? Yep, reduce:

```
array.reduce({}) do |hash, element|
  hash.update(element => true)
end
```

Right off the bat you'll notice that the starting accumulator is a brand new (and empty) hash. If the source array is empty then reduce will return a valid hash instead of the troublesome nil. But when the source array has elements, reduce will invoke the given block once for each element, just like it did in the sum example. Every iteration of the block then adds a key to the hash with true as the associated value. Since the Hash#update method returns the mutated hash, the return value for the block is also a hash. So the requirement that the block return a new accumulator is also satisfied. Awesome!

Converting arrays to hashes using reduce is more space efficient than the version that used map. But it's still not very interesting. Let's use reduce to join together two loops and in the process show off some slightly more complicated logic in the block. Suppose we have an array of users we'd like to filter so the resulting array only includes people who are 21 or older. Then we'd like to convert the array of users into an array of names. Without access to reduce, you'd probably write something like this:

```
users.select {|u| u.age >= 21}.map(&:name)
```

While that certainly works, it's not very efficient. The select method will walk through the entire array of users and return a new array with just those who are 21 or older. This new array is then traversed with map and another new array is returned containing just names. If we use reduce we don't need to create or traverse more than one array:

```
users.reduce([]) do |names, user|
  names << user.name if user.age >= 21
  names
end
```

Do you see a pattern emerging? The block given to reduce can do anything you'd like with the yielded accumulator and elements (including nothing) just so long as it returns a new accumulator. In this example, the block ends by returning the names array. This ensures that the block returns an accumulator even if the conditional logic is false. If no users are 21 or over then reduce will return an empty list. I've said it several times so far but it's worth repeating: Make sure the block always returns an accumulator. Sometimes it might be a completely new accumulator object (like with sum) and other times it's the same accumulator object that was yielded to the block (such as in this example).

Speaking of patterns, you probably write fold-like code all the time without using reduce. Recognizing a fold and then refactoring to use a direct invocation of reduce often leads to simpler, self-contained code. So, what does a fold without reduce look like? Think about the last time you used the each method to iterate though a collection to update a variable. For example, you may have previously converted an array into a hash using code like this:

```
hash = {}

array.each do |element|
  hash[element] = true
end
```

This is precisely the pattern that reduce is meant to help with. When you see a pattern like this in your code consider using reduce to clean it up.

Things to Remember

✦ Always use a starting value for the accumulator.

✦ The block given to reduce should always return an accumulator. It's fine to mutate the current accumulator, just remember to return it from the block.

Item 20: Consider Using a Default Hash Value

You're a Ruby programmer who, I'm sure, has been around the block a few times. So tell me, how often do you see the following pattern show up in code?

```
def frequency (array)
  array.reduce({}) do |hash, element|
    hash[element] ||= 0  # Make sure the key exists.
    hash[element] += 1   # Then increment it.
    hash                 # Return the hash to reduce.
  end
end
```

I'm referring specifically to using the "||=" operator to ensure that a key is set in a hash before attempting to modify it in some way. Why do we have to resort to this? Okay, I know you know the answer, but bear with me for a bit and you might discover that things aren't as straightforward as you think they are. Or maybe they are. Either way, I'd like to show you some alternatives to this pattern.

You already know that if you try to fetch a value from a hash using a nonexistent key you'll get back nil. It's even likely that you've been bitten by this and shoved a few "||" or "||=" operators here and there to get around it. But Hash doesn't return nil because it wants to punish you. It just happens to be the default value, one you're free to change. That's right—you can have Hash return any value you like for nonexistent keys *instead* of nil. I'm not a huge fan of nil, but in this case using it as the default value for hashes makes sense. But when we actually use a hash in our code for a specific purpose, there's often a better default value to be found.

Look at the previous frequency method again. If you could change the default value for the hash used as the accumulator to reduce, what would you choose? The answer's right there on the right-hand side of the "||=" operator.... Take a look at another version of this method, this time using 0 as the default value:

```
def frequency (array)
  array.reduce(Hash.new(0)) do |hash, element|
    hash[element] += 1 # Increment the value.
    hash               # Return the hash to reduce.
  end
end
```

Hey, before you run off and start changing all your hashes let's take a closer look at what's going on. There are a couple of gotchas lurking in the dark. Obviously, the value given to Hash::new becomes the default value for the hash. But keep in mind that the default value is only used when you try to access nonexistent keys. It doesn't magically populate the hash when you attempt to read from it. This is a really important detail about hashes and default values. Consider this IRB session:

```
irb> h = Hash.new(42)

irb> h[:missing_key]
---> 42

irb> h.keys # Hash is still empty!
---> []

irb> h[:missing_key] += 1
---> 43

irb> h.keys # Ah, there you are.
---> [:missing_key]
```

Notice that accessing a nonexistent key returns the default value *without* modifying the hash. Using the "+=" operator does indeed update the hash as you'd expect, but it's not as clear as it could be. It helps to recall what "+=" expands to:

```
# Short version:
hash[key] += 1
```

```
# Expands to:
hash[key] = hash[key] + 1
```

Now it's clear that the assignment happens by first fetching the default value, then adding one to it, and finally storing the resulting value in the hash under the same key. Also notice that we don't mutate the default value in any way. Sure, the default value in this code is a Fixnum, which isn't mutable, but what happens when we do use a mutable value as the default value and then mutate it? This is where things start to get interesting. Check this out:

```
irb> h = Hash.new([])

irb> h[:missing_key]
---> []

irb> h[:missing_key] << "Hey there!"
---> ["Hey there!"]

irb> h.keys # Wait for it...
---> []

irb> h[:missing_key]
---> ["Hey there!"]
```

What in the world is going on? Well, to be honest, I chose an example with a fair amount of dramatic flair. But that's not to say it's unrealistic; I've actually written silly code like this. There are two things that are obscuring what's going on here, and if you go back through the code, I'm sure you'll see them. The first one is simple. Hash::new takes an object to use as the default value. I've given it an empty array. Technically, it's a reference to a mutable array. So if the default value is modified the mutation will be visible each time you request a nonexistent key.

The other bit of trickery on my part is the use of the "<<" operator. Can you see it now? I never actually changed the hash. Requesting a nonexistent key returned the empty array that was then changed by inserting a new element. The hash didn't change but the default value did. That's why the keys method reports that the hash is empty but accessing any nonexistent key returns the recently modified default value. If you really want to insert a new element *and* set a key in the hash you need to go a bit further. But watch out—there's another sneaky side effect waiting for you:

```
irb> h = Hash.new([])

irb> h[:weekdays] = h[:weekdays] << "Monday"

irb> h[:months] = h[:months] << "January"

irb> h.keys
---> [:weekdays, :months]

irb> h[:weekdays]
---> ["Monday", "January"]

irb> h.default
---> ["Monday", "January"]
```

Oh yeah, both keys share the *same* default array, which is probably not what you want to do in most situations. What we'd really like is for the hash to return a brand new array when we access a missing key. It just so happens that there's another way to specify default values for a hash. If you give Hash::new a block it will invoke the block when it needs a default value. Returning a newly created array works nicely:

```
irb> h = Hash.new { [] }

irb> h[:weekdays] = h[:weekdays] << "Monday"

irb> h[:months] = h[:months] << "January"

irb> h[:weekdays]
---> ["Monday"]
```

Much better. But we can take this one step further. The block given to Hash::new can optionally accept two arguments: the hash itself and the key being accessed. That means if we want to mutate the hash we can. Why don't we make it so that accessing a nonexistent key actually sets the key to a new, empty array:

```
irb> h = Hash.new {|hash, key| hash[key] = [] }

irb> h[:weekdays] << "Monday"

irb> h[:holidays]
---> []

irb> h.keys
---> [:weekdays, :holidays]
```

Look familiar? We're back to that tricky code from before, but this time it actually works (with a twist). You can probably see that this technique comes with a major downside. Every time a missing key is accessed, the block will not only create a new entry in the hash, but it'll also create a new array. Let me repeat that: Accessing a nonexistent key will put that key into the hash. This illuminates a problem with default values in general. Let me show you what I mean.

The correct way to check a hash to see if it contains a specific key is with the has_key? method, or one of its aliases. But we're all guilty of exploiting the fact that nil is usually the default value:

```
if hash[key]

  ...

end
```

If the hash has a default value other than nil or false then this con-ditional will *always* succeed. This is a good reminder that it might not be safe to pass a hash with a non-nil default value to a method which isn't expecting it. It should also remind you that checking for the exis-tence of a key by fetching its value is sloppy and won't always do what you expect. Stick to has_key?.

There's another way to work with default values that is sometimes best. The Hash#fetch method works a lot like Hash#[] with a few important changes. Like Hash#[], the first argument to fetch is the key you want to look up in the hash. But fetch can take an optional second argument. If the given key isn't found in the hash then fetch will return its second argument instead. If you omit the second argu-ment then fetch will raise an exception if you attempt to access a non-existent key. This can be a much safer alternative to setting a default value for the entire hash.

```
irb> h = {}

irb> h[:weekdays] = h.fetch(:weekdays, []) << "Monday"
---> ["Monday"]

irb> h.fetch(:missing_key)
KeyError: key not found: :missing_key
```

Using fetch is a bit more verbose but it has its merits. If you need to pass a hash around to code that assumes invalid keys return nil, using fetch is safer than using a default value. But don't discount default values, especially the block version of Hash::new. You can do some really interesting and powerful stuff with both default values and default blocks.

Things to Remember

+ Consider using a default Hash value.

+ Use has_key? or one of its aliases to check if a hash contains a key. That is, don't assume that accessing a nonexistent key will return nil.

+ Don't use default values if you need to pass the hash to code that assumes invalid keys return nil.

+ Hash#fetch can sometimes be a safer alternative to default values.

Item 21: Prefer Delegation to Inheriting from Collection Classes

This item could just as well have been titled "Prefer Delegation to Inheriting from Core Classes" because it applies equally to all of the core Ruby classes. But beginner and intermediate Ruby programmers tend to be more tempted to subclass the collection classes than classes like Fixnum. That's because the collection classes tend to look like good foundations when you want to write your own collection class. If you squint a bit it might even look like this models the "is-a" relationship, which is often promoted as a good basis for using inheritance.

But more often the relationship is truly a "has-a" (composition) relationship that is being shoehorned into an inheritance hierarchy. But I'm not here to rehash the "is-a"/"has-a" debate, there are plenty of other books and papers that have done a much better job on that subject than I could do here. Even if you think you have the most perfect "is-a" relationship with one of the core collection classes, I'm here to tell you why it's a bad idea and show you how to model your classes properly. So, what could possibly be wrong with inheriting from one of the collection classes? For starters, think about the relationship inheritance creates. The subclass first and foremost inherits the public interface from its superclass. This automatically shows up in the documentation and reflection information for your class. In other words, programmers using your class will have the expectation that all those superclass methods will work correctly on your subclass. And that's where we start to run into trouble.

As you know, all of the core Ruby classes are implemented in C. The reason I point this out is because the instance methods for some of these classes don't always respect subclasses. Take the Array#reverse method, for example. Instead of mutating the receiver it returns a new Array. Guess what happens if you subclass Array and use the reverse method on an instance of your subclass? Okay...you don't have to guess—I'll show you:

```
irb> class LikeArray < Array; end

irb> x = LikeArray.new([1, 2, 3])
---> [1, 2, 3]

irb> y = x.reverse
---> [3, 2, 1]

irb> y.class
---> Array
```

Yep, LikeArray#reverse returns an Array and not a LikeArray. But you can't really blame the Array class. The documentation clearly says that reverse returns a new Array. It's just not what you'd like to happen, and it might surprise users of your class. But of course, it doesn't end there; a lot of other instance methods on the collection classes do this. The inherited comparison operators might be even worse. They allow instances of your subclass to be compared with instances of the superclass. Does this make sense?

```
irb> LikeArray.new([1,2,3]) == [1, 2, 3]
---> true
```

Inheritance isn't always the best option in Ruby. Inheriting from the core collection classes almost never makes sense. So what do you do instead? Well, we don't even have to look outside of Ruby's standard library to see an example of how to do this correctly. The Set class is written in Ruby and has a rather simple implementation. It keeps a Hash as its only instance variable and uses it as a place to store elements, forwarding most of its methods on to the hash.

This is a great example of where it might be tempting to have Set inherit from Hash. The Set class implements a lot of the same methods as Hash after all. But a Set isn't a Hash, and we certainly don't want to call a method on a Set and accidentally get back a Hash. That would be weird. So Set takes the "has-a" approach and uses a hash internally without ever exposing it. You don't need to know anything about Hash to use Set. It's just an implementation detail.

But what about classes that really do seem to model the "is-a" relationship? Without being able to inherit from one of the collection classes you might be left writing *a lot* of wrapper methods to expose a similar interface. That's where delegation comes in.

Delegation allows you to declare methods that should be forwarded along to a specific instance variable. It's sort of like using inheritance but with quite a bit more control. With delegation you can expose an interface similar to one of the collection classes without exposing the entire interface. I like to think of delegation as building up a class from external pieces as opposed to tearing out the parts you inherited but don't want. An example is in order here.

Let's write a class based on Hash with one important difference—accessing nonexistent keys raises an exception. There are many different ways to implement something like this, but writing a new class lets us reuse the same implementation easily. Instead of inheriting from Hash and then putting bandages all over the code to make sure it works correctly we'll use delegation. We'll only need one instance variable, @hash, which does all the heavy lifting for us. Let's create the class and set up delegation to @hash:

```
require('forwardable')

class RaisingHash
  extend(Forwardable)
  include(Enumerable)
  def_delegators(:@hash, :[], :[]=, :delete, :each,
                         :keys, :values, :length,
                         :empty?, :has_key?)
end
```

There are several ways to implement delegation in Ruby. The Forwardable module makes it easy to delegate the listed methods to a specific instance variable. It's part of the standard library (and not the Ruby core library), which is why we need require.

After extending the Forwardable module you can use the def_delegators class method. The first argument should be a symbol representing the name of an instance variable to use as the target object. But the target doesn't have to be an instance variable. If the symbol given to def_delegators is the name of a method, that will work too. In this case, the method should return an object that will then be used as the delegation target. The remaining arguments to def_delegators are names of instance methods that should be forwarded to the target object. This is a lot like using the attr_accessor method to generate getter and setter methods. For delegation, the def_delegators method will generate instance methods that simply forward the requested message to the target object.

This is where using delegation instead of inheritance really starts to shine. Using def_delegators we specifically choose which hash methods we want to expose through the RaisingHash public interface. Since we're going to raise exceptions for missing keys it doesn't really make sense to support the Hash#fetch method. If we were using inheritance we'd have to hide unwanted methods with undef_method or mark them as private. With delegation we cherry pick the methods we want to support. We can even take this a bit further.

Using def_delegators assumes you want to name the locally generated instance method the same as the delegation target's method. In other words, delegating the delete method creates a RaisingHash#delete method that forwards the message to @hash.delete. But sometimes you want to use a different local name. You can do this with the def_delegator method. For example, if you wanted the RaisingHash#erase! method forwarded to @hash.delete you'd use the following def_delegator call:

```
# Forward self.erase! to @hash.delete
def_delegator(:@hash, :delete, :erase!)
```

After setting up the delegation methods you need to make sure that the initialize method creates the instance variable mentioned in the delegation declarations. This step requires a bit more work on our RaisingHash class. Remember that we want to raise exceptions when an invalid key is used with the hash. While we could certainly write our own "[]" operator that verifies each access, there's a simpler way. Let's use the technique from Item 20 and give Hash::new a block that just raises a KeyError. Since the block is only ever called when a nonexistent key is accessed, we don't have to perform any key-checking logic. This also means that if we expose any other methods for access keys in the hash we don't have to duplicate the KeyError raising code. Here's the initialize method:

```
def initialize
  @hash = Hash.new do |hash, key|
    raise(KeyError, "invalid key '#{key}'!")
  end
end
```

At this point you could create a new RaisingHash object and see that the delegation works as expected. But you may have noticed that there are several Hash methods we aren't delegating to @hash. As I mentioned earlier, not all of the Hash methods make sense for RaisingHash, but there's another reason too. Delegation isn't the correct answer for all methods. Remember the methods I mentioned earlier that return a new Hash instead of the proper subclass? Just as with inheritance we need to deal with those carefully. Hash#invert is one such method, so we need to implement our own version that ensures that a new RaisingHash is returned instead of a Hash:

```
def invert
  other = self.class.new
  other.replace!(@hash.invert)
  other
end
```

```
protected
def replace! (hash)
  hash.default_proc = @hash.default_proc
  @hash = hash
end
```

Notice that RaisingHash#invert used the protected method replace! to update the @hash instance variable in the other RaisingHash object. This technique comes from Item 14 and establishes the replace! method as a gateway for changing the @hash variable for other internal methods. The replace! method isolates an important piece of logic, ensuring that any hash assigned to @hash uses the same default_proc. So what is a default_proc and why is it important?

The default_proc for a Hash is the block given to the Hash::new method and is supposed to return a default value, but in our case it raises an exception. As it turns out, Hash methods that return a brand new hash (such as invert) don't copy the default_proc into the new hash. If the return value from Hash#invert was directly placed into the @hash instance variable then accessing an invalid key would no longer raise an exception. So we need to ensure that the block that was used in the initialize method is copied into the incoming hash. This preserves the logic that raises KeyError exceptions.

There's one last set of considerations for the RaisingHash class. Because it's pretending to be a collection class (all the real logic is in @hash) we need to make sure it behaves correctly when duplicated or cloned. It also needs to properly respond to the freeze, taint, and untaint methods. Let's start with dup and clone.

If someone duplicates a RaisingHash object Ruby will, by default, create a new object that has instance variables identical to the original object. Since the @hash instance variable is the real container, we need to arrange to have it duplicated as well. This logic belongs in the initialize_copy method, which is called just after a new object is created from an original:

```
def initialize_copy (other)
  @hash = @hash.dup
end
```

The receiver of the initialize_copy method is the new object and it's given the original object as its only argument. When initialize_copy is called all of the instance variables point to the ones from the original object. We only need to duplicate the @hash variable. Pretty simple.

Finally, we come to freezing and tainting. Since RaisingHash is delegating mutating methods to @hash we need to ensure that if an instance of RaisingHash is frozen so is its @hash instance variable. Fortunately,

overriding the freeze method is straightforward. We just need to pass
the message on to @hash and then call super:

```
def freeze
  @hash.freeze
  super
end
```

The taint and untaint methods should behave the same way. That is,
they should pass the message on to @hash and then call super. With
those methods in place, freezing, tainting, or untainting a RaisingHash
object also affects the internal hash object. If we didn't do this then
a mutating method like delete would continue to work even with a
frozen RaisingHash object. That's not how freezing should work. Make
sure you take this into consideration.

Things to Remember

✦ Prefer delegation to inheriting from collection classes.

✦ Don't forget to write an initialize_copy method that duplicates the
  delegation target.

✦ Write freeze, taint, and untaint methods that send the corresponding message to the delegation target followed by a call to super.

Exceptions

Sometimes an error condition is bad enough that it seems flat-out rude to return nil from a method. When things get this mucked up it's best to unwind the stack and provide details describing the failure.

Purists (of which I'm a card-carrying member) believe that exceptions should rarely be used...mostly to give a meaningful apology to the user (followed promptly by crashing the program and discarding all her hard work).

Ruby programmers tend to be more liberal with exceptions. A number of routine error conditions are encoded into standard exception classes and used to report specific failures. Fortunately, the most common exception classes contain enough information that it's practical to rescue the exception and recover from the error condition.

Exceptions and exception handling are a complicated business. They interrupt the normal control flow of a program, acting like a sort of broken time machine. They're computationally expensive, and they're mentally laborious for programmers. "Where's that exception going to end up?"

My goal for this chapter is to show you how to avoid common problems with exceptions and how to use them properly. More importantly, you'll learn to write code that can safely coexist in the presence of exceptions.

Item 22: Prefer Custom Exceptions to Raising Strings

Suppose you're writing a library and a particular method might encounter an error condition. After thinking on it for a great deal of time you've decided that this error warrants an exception. Which exception do you raise? What details do you include in the exception?

Exceptions can be thought of as two different language features rolled into one: error descriptions and control flow. This item is concerned with the former, while the latter is covered in Items 26 and 27.

Primarily, an exception is an object that contains information about an error condition. Most often, that information is simply a human readable description of the error that is printed to the terminal just before the program crashes. But, as you know, that's not the only thing you can do with exceptions. They can be intercepted and handled with a rescue clause.

Certain types of exceptions represent errors that can be recovered from. Sometimes that means you abort the current task and log an error message. More detailed exceptions might allow you to change the state of the program and try the operation again. A network timeout, for example, might raise an exception that would trigger a short delay followed by a retry.

In order to recover from a failure you need to be able to differentiate the various possible error conditions. Unfortunately, Ruby makes it too easy to be lazy with exceptions. A much too common practice among Ruby programmers is to use raise with a String:

```
raise("coffee machine low on water")
```

Recall that the raise method in Ruby comes in several flavors. When given a single argument, and that argument is a string, raise will create a RuntimeError using the string as the error message. It's equivalent to the more explicit:

```
raise(RuntimeError, "coffee machine low on water")
```

As you can see, instead of using a string you can supply a class name as the first argument to raise. In this case, it will create an exception object from the class and then raise that object. The second (and optional) argument is the string to use as the error message. Without an explicit error message the name of the class will be used (which isn't very useful as far as error messages go).

Raising a RuntimeError might be fine if you intend to terminate the program. For anything else, it isn't very useful. A RuntimeError is nothing more than a generic "Oops, something went wrong" error. Because you're writing code for other programmers to use, a RuntimeError is a poor choice, and by extension so is raising a string.

If you're bound and determined to raise an exception, then you should create a new class for it. Since exceptions are handled based on their type, creating a new class is the standard way to differentiate it.

Creating a new exception class is trivial. You only need to consider three rules:

- New exception classes must inherit from one of the standard exception classes. Attempting to raise anything else will result in a TypeError (discarding the exception you were trying to raise in the first place).

- The standard exception classes form a hierarchy with the Exception base class as the root. But Exception and several of its subclasses are considered low-level errors that will generally crash the program. The majority of the standard exception classes inherit instead from StandardError and you should follow suit.

- While not technically a requirement, it's common practice to add the "Error" suffix to exception class names.

Another reason to inherit from StandardError comes from the default behavior of the rescue clause. As you know, you can omit the class name when handling exceptions with rescue. In this case, it will intercept any exception whose class (or superclass) is StandardError. (The same is true when you use rescue as a statement modifier.)

Custom exception classes can be as simple or as complicated as you'd like. They're just classes after all. Let's start with something simple (the more common case) and work our way up to a slightly more complicated situation. As recommended, we'll create a class that inherits from StandardError. Not surprisingly, all the functionality we need is already baked in to the Exception class and passed down to our new class for free when we inherit from StandardError:

```
class CoffeeTooWeakError < StandardError; end
```

With a custom exception class, errors can now be uniquely identified. People using your code gain the ability to choose how they want to handle (or not handle) these types of errors, and you've made the world a slightly better place. I congratulate you...but stay with me for a few more paragraphs—you still need to put this hard work into action and actually use this new exception class. Doing so is exactly like using any other exception:

```
raise(CoffeeTooWeakError)
```

Preferably you'd supply an error message to go along with the exception. Otherwise, a rather useless message will show up on the console if the program ends in a fiery death. A little extra information can go a long way:

```
raise(CoffeeTooWeakError, "coffee to water ratio too low")
```

And there you have it. This short, two-line enhancement provides a wealth of information for other programmers. Can you imagine going back to simply raising strings? I sure hope not.

Now that I've got you hooked on customizing exceptions you're probably wondering how you can make them even more useful. Maybe you'd like to provide more detail than just an error message. Perhaps some additional information attached to the exception would help programmers using your code decide how to proceed when handling these exceptions. Adding that additional information is simple. Remember, these are just plain Ruby classes. Let's create another exception class, this time demonstrating how to report this extra information along with the error message.

Suppose you're working on a utility that drives the operation of a 3D printer. The temperature of the printer needs to be within a specific range to function properly. You've decided that if the temperature is out of range you'll raise an exception, but you don't want to report the current temperature buried somewhere within an error message. It would be nice if the temperature could be programmatically extracted from the exception. The code handling the exception could then change the color of the error message on the printer's screen to reflect if it's too cold or too hot.

Writing the custom exception class is straightforward. We'll capture the temperature in an instance variable and then generate an error message for the exception using the temperature value:

```ruby
class TemperatureError < StandardError
  attr_reader(:temperature)

  def initialize (temperature)
    @temperature = temperature
    super("invalid temperature: #@temperature")
  end
end
```

Nothing really special here. Just remember to initialize the base class with a call to super so the upstream Exception class can set up some internal instance variables, including the error message. As before, the next step is to put our new exception class to work. But this time, things are slightly different:

```ruby
raise(TemperatureError.new(180))
```

Instead of using a class name with raise we're giving it an exception *object*. Clearly, we need to create the exception object ourselves to pass in the temperature, so giving raise a class name isn't an option. Fortunately, raise is smart enough to accept either a class or an object. Ignoring the special case of raise where you give it a string, it's worthwhile to briefly explore how it creates an exception from the object you give it.

The raise method doesn't do any voodoo or introspection with its first argument; it simply sends it a message (the exception message to be more specific). This method is supposed to return an object that can then be raised. Both exception classes and exception objects have their own exception method courtesy of the Exception class. The class method version is simply an alias for new and isn't very interesting. So passing a class to raise causes it to call new on the class (via the exception method) and raise the resulting object.

But the instance method version of exception is a bit weird, depending on how many arguments are given to raise:

- In the single-argument version of raise (the one we used above), the exception method is invoked with no arguments. With no arguments, the exception method simply returns self without doing anything. This short-circuit behavior means that the object given to raise as its first argument becomes the raised exception.

- But if you provide raise with an exception object *and* an error message it will invoke the exception method with a single argument—the error message. In this case, the exception method will make a copy of the exception, reset its error message to the one given, and then return the copy. This results in the copy (along with the new error message) being raised instead.

Keep this second case in mind if you're setting the error message in the initialize method like we did above. Giving raise one of our TemperatureError objects *and* an error message will result in the error message from initialize being overwritten. When working with exceptions that generate their own error messages you should use the single-argument version of raise instead. (Unless, of course, your goal is to actually overwrite the error message.)

Armed with the rules for creating custom exception classes you're ready to make all of your errors more descriptive and useful. But before I turn you loose I'd like to make one final recommendation.

If you find yourself creating several exception classes for a single project you should consider arranging them in their own class hierarchy. That is, designate one of them as a base class the remaining classes inherit from. The base class should, of course, inherit from StandardError. Structuring your exception classes this way gives other programmers even more flexibility when handling your exceptions.

Things to Remember

✦ Avoid raising strings as exceptions; they're converted into generic `RuntimeError` objects. Create a custom exception class instead.

✦ Custom exception classes should inherit from `StandardError` and use the "Error" suffix in their class name.

✦ When creating more than one exception class for a project, start by creating a base class that inherits from `StandardError`. Other exception classes should inherit from this custom base class.

✦ If you write an `initialize` method for your custom exception class make sure to call super, preferably with an error message.

✦ When setting an error message in `initialize`, keep in mind that setting an error message with `raise` will take precedence over the one in `initialize`.

Item 23: Rescue the Most Specific Exception Possible

So you're working on a critical piece of software that needs to have the minimum amount of downtime. Since it runs in the real world it's not uncommon for the application to experience a variety of errors—everything from network connection failures to corrupt data in the database conspire against your plan to write a robust program. So you decide to handle exceptions as much as possible instead of letting the program crash. Because different exceptions might be raised while performing a crucial task, wrapping the task in a `begin` block seems like the obvious way to go:

```
begin
  task.perform
rescue => e
  logger.error("task failed: #{e}")
  # Swallow exception, abort task.
end
```

Realizing that using rescue without a class name is a rather large net, you decide to at least log the error message before swallowing the exception. But just how wide is this net?

As you know, using rescue like this is a shortcut for rescuing `StandardError` and any of its subclasses. The problem is that this just happens to be the majority of the exception classes. These are the so-called "high-level" exceptions that are safe to handle and sometimes ignored. But among them are exceptions related to your source code as well. Exceptions like `LocalJumpError` and `ArgumentError` aren't environmental issues like the network or file system—they're errors caused by mistakes in the code.

Perhaps they're mistakes such as forgetting to validate a user entry before using it, but they're mistakes nonetheless. You really don't want to cover up these sorts of errors by grouping them with other StandardError exceptions. You also don't want to specifically list them all out and deal with them individually. You can think of it as a black-list vs. whitelist issue.

Blacklisting is inclusive—everything is allowed unless specifically denied. Dealing with exceptions this way would have you first list-ing out all the exceptions you *don't* want to handle, simply re-raising them immediately after being rescued. The final rescue clause is then your "everything else" bucket. Obviously, this is a nightmare:

```
begin
  task.perform
rescue ArgumentError, LocalJumpError,
       NoMethodError, ZeroDivisionError
  # Don't actually handle these.
  raise
rescue => e
  logger.error("task failed: #{e}")
  # Swallow exception, abort task.
end
```

If you follow the blacklist pattern you need to list the exceptions like this because Ruby evaluates the rescue clauses in order, from top to bottom, and first match wins. That means if you rescue StandardError before LocalJumpError the more generic (higher in the class hierarchy) StandardError would always win. Furthermore, the code no longer clearly represents your intention. Someone working on this code in a few months may see these rescue statements as redundant and remove them. In other words, this style is too brittle and error-prone. What can you do?

A more natural approach would be to rescue only those specific excep-tions you know how to handle and let the rest propagate up the stack. This is more like whitelisting, where everything is denied unless spe-cifically allowed (exclusive). This method requires you to spend more time considering potential error conditions but with the benefit that they are handled with specific solutions.

Suppose you know that the two most common errors your code will encounter will be network connection failures and invalid database records. Connection failures can be handled by retrying after a delay for a set number of times before giving up. (Make sure you heed the advice in Item 26 when using the `retry` statement.) The bad records, on the other hand, need to be flagged and sent off to support staff.

Item 22 recommends that you have specific exception classes for these two types of errors, and this is precisely the reason why:

```
begin
  task.perform
rescue NetworkConnectionError => e
  # Retry logic...
rescue InvalidRecordError => e
  # Send record to support staff...
end
```

With dedicated exception classes it's straightforward to rescue specific errors and deal with them individually. This way the common error conditions are taken care of and the generic (and hopefully rare) errors continue on their way toward eventually crashing the program.

If you still feel like you want that catchall bucket at the end of the rescue chain you might actually be itching for an ensure clause. This is especially true if you just want to perform some housecleaning before a raised exception causes the current scope to exit. Since the ensure clause will execute for both normal and exceptional situations it's the preferred way to clean up. Items 24 and 25 provide some recommendations for using ensure correctly.

Still want to use a general-purpose `rescue`? Okay, I'll admit that you might occasionally have a genuine reason to rescue generic exceptions. For example, when you want to send the details of the exception to a remote monitoring service before re-raising it:

```
begin
  task.perform
rescue NetworkConnectionError => e
  # Retry logic...
rescue InvalidRecordError => e
  # Send record to support staff...
rescue => e
  service.record(e)
  raise
ensure
  ...
end
```

I'd be remiss if I didn't mention a not-so-insignificant detail about rescuing exceptions. While it's completely admirable and highly recommended to handle recoverable exceptions, it's not without its fair share of risk. Consider the example above where invalid database records trigger exceptions that are subsequently rescued and then sent off to the support team. Suppose this process involves making a network connection to the support system and transmitting the details of the invalid record. What happens if there's a network connection failure while connecting to this other system? I'll say this: It's not pretty.

Exceptions raised while a rescue clause is executing replace the original exception, exit the scope of the rescue clause, and start exception processing with the *new* exception. This isn't ideal since the original reason you were handling an exception has been lost and instead some other exception is parading around in its place. This is especially egregious if the lost exception is something like LocalJumpError, which was accidentally rescued by a generic rescue clause such as the one above that sends exceptions to some reporting service. Ouch.

This can be mitigated by performing any recovery work in a dedicated method that receives the original exception as an argument. Any exceptions that occur in the method can be handled by raising the original exception:

```
def send_to_support_staff (e)
  ...
rescue
  raise(e)
end
```

Of course, this assumes the original exception is more important than the exception raised during the recovery process. Going to such lengths is a call you'll have to make on your own.

Things to Remember

+ Rescue only those specific exceptions from which you know how to recover.

+ When rescuing an exception, handle the most specific type first. The higher a class is in the exception hierarchy the lower it should be in your chain of rescue clauses.

+ Avoid rescuing generic exception classes such as StandardError. If you find yourself doing this you should consider whether what you really want is an ensure clause instead.

+ Raising an exception from a rescue clause will replace the current exception and immediately leave the current scope, resuming exception processing.

Item 24: **Manage Resources with Blocks and** ensure

As you know, Ruby includes a garbage collector so you can be a happy programmer and avoid manual memory management. For example, you can slurp a large file into memory without worrying that a raised exception will result in a memory leak.

"But what about other types of resources besides memory?" you ask. That's a good question. I'm glad you're thinking ahead.

There are a variety of resources that are not handled by the garbage collector, yet like precious bytes of memory, these resources make use of the allocate-use-release pattern. Database connections, temporary files, and file locks are all good examples of resources that must eventually be freed.

Releasing a resource when you've finished with it seems easy enough. But exceptions are the ultimate monkey wrench when it comes to resource management. Consider this code:

```
file = File.open(file_name, 'w')
...
file.close
```

What happens when an exception is raised before the file is closed? The good news is that the File class leverages the garbage collector as described in Item 45, so the file will eventually be closed. The "eventually" part is the problem.

If you rely on the garbage collector you should know that there are no guarantees about *when* a resource will be released, only that it will happen sometime in the future. (And possibly not at all if you accidentally maintain a reference to the resource.) While the garbage collector is great at what it does, most resources need to be released in a timely fashion.

When working with files there is a limit on the maximum number that can be concurrently open. Depending on the operating system this upper limit might be shared with network connections as well. So it's clearly more desirable to close the file immediately after you're done with it than wait for the garbage collector. Fortunately, there's a better way to manage resources, and it works even if exceptions are raised.

The trick is to use the begin keyword to create a new scope for exceptions. You can then add an ensure clause to release the resource whether any exceptions are raised or not.

The beauty of the ensure clause is that its body will be executed for both normal and exceptional situations. An exception-safe way to use a file isn't much more complicated than what we've seen before:

```
begin
  file = File.open(file_name, 'w')
  ...
ensure
  file.close if file
end
```

If an exception is raised anywhere in the body of the begin block, the file will be closed by the ensure clause. Since the ensure clause also executes when the begin body finishes successfully, you know the file will be closed in all possible outcomes.

In addition, expressions in the ensure clause are executed within the same scope as the begin body. Variables defined there are also available in the ensure clause. But exercise caution—it's possible that they haven't been initialized yet. That's the reason I've made the call to file.close conditional.

It's possible that File.open failed and raised an exception. In such a case, the ensure clause will still run even though the file was never opened. In an ensure clause it's a good idea to check if a variable is initialized before attempting to use it. Uninitialized variables in this context will always be nil.

While this code fits the bill for safely managing resources in the presence of exceptions, it's a bit cumbersome to write repeatedly. Ideally, we'd like to be able to abstract away this responsibility.

It just so happens that there's a design idiom in Ruby that makes resource management fairly painless. To see an example of this idiom in practice we don't have to look any further than File::open:

```
File.open(file_name, 'w') do |file|
  ...
end
```

Given a block, the File::open method opens the file as it did before. But this time, the file will be yielded to the block and when the block finishes the file will be closed. The file is only open as long as it's needed.

As you probably guessed, the file is closed using an ensure clause. So if the body of the block raises an exception, the file will still be closed.

Writing code in this style is fairly straightforward. If a method is associated with a block you can use the yield statement to invoke the block and pass in the newly acquired resource:

```
class Lock
  def self.acquire
```

```
      lock = new   # Initialize the resource
      lock.exclusive_lock!
      yield(lock) # Give it to the block
    ensure
      # Make sure it gets unlocked.
      lock.unlock if lock
    end
  end
end
```

Using this class is equivalent to the File example:

```
Lock.acquire do |lock|
  # Raising an exception here is okay.
end
```

I'm sure you'd agree that it would be nicer if Lock::acquire could be used exactly like File::open. That is, if given a block the method will own the resource and ensure it's released. Without a block it simply returns the resource and the caller is responsible for sending the unlock message. (Hopefully employing ensure in the process.)

We only need one more helper method to make this work. The block_given? method returns true if a block is associated with the method. With this in hand, we can extend Lock::acquire to behave in the same way that File::open does:

```
class Lock
  def self.acquire
    lock = new # Initialize the resource.
    lock.exclusive_lock!

    if block_given?
      yield(lock)
    else
      lock # Act more like Lock::new.
    end
  ensure
    if block_given?
      # Make sure it gets unlocked.
      lock.unlock if lock
    end
  end
end
```

Without an associated block, Lock::acquire will now simply return the lock and won't attempt to automatically unlock it.

```
lock = Lock.acquire
# Won't automatically unlock.
```

What I really like about this abstraction is that it's not difficult to write, and once it's in place it performs an important job silently behind the scenes. If I allocate a resource and then leave the current scope through normal control flow or due to an exception, the resource will always be released.

Things to Remember

+ Write an ensure clause to release any acquired resources.

+ Use the block and ensure pattern with a class method to abstract away resource management.

+ Make sure variables are initialized before using them in an ensure clause.

Item 25: Exit ensure Clauses by Flowing Off the End

Item 24 makes the point that using an ensure clause is the best way to manage resources in the presence of exceptions. More generally, ensure can be used to perform any sort of housekeeping before leaving the current scope. It's a fantastic, general-purpose cleaning product. But like any useful tool, ensure comes with a warning label and some sharp edges.

Being closely related to rescue clauses, it should come as no surprise that ensure can fulfill some of the same duties as rescue. Of course, this is limited to when an ensure clause is executing due to a propagating exception (which is only one of the reasons it might be executing).

One of the features that both rescue and ensure share is the ability to terminate exception processing. You already know that rescue catches exceptions. From within rescue you can choose to cancel propagation and deal with the error, resuming normal control flow. You can also restart exception processing by raising the original exception or by creating a new one.

With rescue, terminating exception handling is explicit. The fact that a rescue clause is present tells you that an exception is going to be dropped or dealt with. On the other hand, ensure gives you warm fuzzies about cleaning up and preventing resource leaks.

You probably don't expect that an ensure clause can alter control flow and swallow exceptions. That's certainly not its primary purpose. Nevertheless, it's possible, fairly simple, and slightly subtle. All it takes is an explicit return statement:

```
def tricky
  ...
  return 'horses'
```

```
ensure
  return 'ponies'
end
```

Since there are two reasons why an ensure clause executes, we need to understand how the code above affects both. Let's first look at the exceptional situation.

Suppose for a moment that from the depths of the call stack an exception is making its way upward. Wisely, you've written an ensure clause to clean up after yourself. But strangely enough, you've also written a return statement in the ensure clause. Why in the world would you do that?

What will happen when the executing ensure clause reaches the return statement? The exception is discarded and the enclosing method returns as normal. Its return value is replaced with the return value from the ensure clause. This would make perfect sense if it weren't absolutely horrible.

"You shouldn't catch exceptions that you can't properly handle," you say. I agree! That's what makes this so heinous.

Item 23 advises that you should only rescue the exceptions you can handle. Returning from ensure directly discards that advice with some unfortunate consequences. Used this way, the ensure clause turns into the Bermuda Triangle for exceptions.

To illustrate how undesirable this is we'll need to compare it to rescue. Using an explicit return inside ensure is *close* to writing a bare rescue:

```
def hammer
  ...
  return 'hit'
rescue
  # Discard exceptions.
  return 'smash'
end
```

When you don't specify which exceptions you intend to intercept you are opting for the default set, which is StandardError and its children. More importantly, it means there are several other exception classes that won't be caught. That's a good thing.

There are plenty of exceptions you shouldn't catch. How do you handle SyntaxError or NoMemoryError? You don't. You simply clean up and let the exception continue. Hopefully, code further up the stack knows what to do with those.

Let's get back to that return statement in ensure. The reason it's worse than a bare rescue is that it will discard *any* exception. Let me repeat that: It completely throws away *any* type of exception. It's a pretty big hammer. Avoid using it.

Instead, clearly show your intent with a proper `rescue`:

```
def explicit
  ...
  return 'horses'
rescue SpecificError => e
  # Recover from the exception.
  return 'ponies'
ensure
  # Clean up only.
end
```

This is probably what you meant to write anyway. Furthermore, the code above doesn't suffer from the problems created when ensure is executing due to normal (nonexceptional) flow. If you've been keeping track you've probably noticed that we haven't covered that situation yet.

Take another look at the problem code from the beginning of this item:

```
def tricky
  ...
  return 'horses'
ensure
  return 'ponies'
end
```

This time let's consider what happens when no exceptions are raised. You might call this the "happy path," since the method finishes successfully and returns a value. This is the second reason an ensure clause will run.

Do you remember that pesky `return` statement you wrote into the ensure clause? When it executes this time it simply takes over the return value of the method. From the outside it appears that the method returned normally and with the value from the ensure clause. Talk about obfuscation.

Notice that for all outcomes this method will *always* return the value from the ensure clause and never the main body. This is subtly different than the `hammer` method above. It only returns 'smash' when an exception occurs. Otherwise, the body's return value is maintained.

Even if you think you have a good reason to do something like this, you should reconsider. The same result can be achieved using conditionals in the body of the method or in a `rescue` clause. It's safer and more clearly shows your intention.

Up until this point we've focused heavily on the return statement. But as you know, it's not the only way to exit the current scope. There's an even more powerful keyword than return. The throw statement can be a powerful ally when it comes to control flow. (Item 27 points out why throw should be used instead of raise for control flow.)

Obviously, using throw inside ensure has all the same problems as return. What might not be as obvious are the keywords that alter the flow of iterations and loops. Specifically, next and break. Consider what happens when you place them inside ensure:

```ruby
items.each do |item|
  begin
    raise TooStrongError if item == 'lilac'
  ensure
    next # Cancels exception, continues iteration.
  end
end
```

Used this way, next and break can silently discard exceptions. By now we should agree that if you're going to throw away exceptions it should be done inside a rescue clause where it belongs. (Oh, and you have a really good reason to do so.)

Things to Remember

✦ Avoid using explicit return statements from within ensure clauses. This suggests there's something wrong with the logic in the method body.

✦ Similarly, don't use throw directly inside ensure. You probably meant to place throw in the body of the method.

✦ When iterating, never use next or break in an ensure clause. Ask yourself if you actually need the begin block inside the iteration. It might make more sense to invert the relationship, placing the iteration inside the begin.

✦ More generally, don't alter control flow in an ensure clause. Do that in a rescue clause instead. Your intent will be much clearer.

Item 26: Bound retry Attempts, Vary Their Frequency, and Keep an Audit Trail

Item 23 explains why it's important to rescue only those specific exceptions you know how to handle and how things can go wrong when using rescue. I recommend you familiarize yourself with the ramifications involved when using rescue because this item expands on that idea by demonstrating how to resolve an error condition by rerunning the code that caused it.

Although not very common, certain errors can be safely handled by rescuing the resulting exception and restarting the enclosing scope with the retry keyword. Suppose you've written a program that communicates with a third-party vendor using a fancy web API. When specific records in your database change your code kicks off and attempts to transmit the changes to the vendor. The only problem is the vendor is running some very buggy software. One out of every 30 requests you make results in a response informing you that your data transfer failed due to a database deadlock error. But the good news is the vendor is aware of the problem and should have it fixed in the next three months.

After some experimenting you discover a simple workaround. Retrying the request after a short delay results in a successful transaction. With hundreds of these failures an hour, this task clearly needs to be automated. A natural first attempt might look something like this:

```
begin
  service.update(record)
rescue VendorDeadlockError
  sleep(15)
  retry
end
```

But there's a major problem with this code that isn't immediately obvious. Testing this code—even putting it into production—might work in the short term, until an unexpected edge case is encountered. The problem lies with how we're using retry and the fact that it creates a hidden loop in the code. As long as the update method continues to raise a VendorDeadlockError the block will continue to get restarted. Writing an unconditional retry is akin to writing an infinite loop. To make this easier to understand consider this use of while, which emulates our first attempt without using retry:

```
while true
  begin
    service.update(record)
  rescue VendorDeadlockError
    sleep(15)
    # Drop exception
  else
    break # Success, exit loop.
  end
end
```

This is much uglier, but it does make the loop explicit. If we're going to use `retry` then we need to take this implicit loop into consideration. One correct solution is to place an upper bound on the number of retry attempts. This is often done with a bounding variable. The tricky part is ensuring that this variable is correctly scoped:

```
retries = 0

begin
  service.update(record)
rescue VendorDeadlockError
  raise if retries >= 3
  retries += 1
  sleep(15)
  retry
end
```

Notice that the `retries` variable is defined and initialized *outside* of the `begin` block. Had it been initialized inside instead it would continually reset to 0 each time `retry` restarted the `begin` block, invalidating the bounds checking and creating a potentially infinite loop. Getting the scoping correct for the bounding variable is simple when you think about it, but it's easy to miss if you haven't used `retry` before or forget about the invisible loop.

Another big improvement with the above refinement is the action taken when the number of allowed retries has been exceeded. You know it's taboo to swallow and ignore an exception, so after we've tried a reasonable number of times to resolve the error the best course of action is to re-raise the exception. We've done what we can and the right thing to do is to bid the exception farewell and send it off to be dealt with higher up in the call stack.

But there are still a couple of changes we can make to our code so the recovery effort is even more robust. First off, we don't want `retry` to cover up the fact that an exception was raised. If retrying the failed code finally ends in success then it's probably not a big deal if the original exception is discarded.

On the other hand, consider what happens when you `retry` and the result is another failure, but with a different exception. To the outside world the first exception never happened...only the second. That might lead to a late-night debugging session trying to figure out the chain of events that led to the failure. Preferably you'd leave some breadcrumbs for yourself to follow in such an event. This can be as simple as writing the exception to a log file before invoking `retry` or as complicated as writing failure events to a database.

Whichever approach you take it's definitely a good idea to record the fact that an exception happened before you use retry. At the very least, you'll be able to figure out how often the temperamental code is failing.

The final addition to our example has to do with the frequency at which we retry failed code. It's unreasonable to think that immediately retrying the transaction will succeed, which is why we have the short delay already in place. But if we keep making a request to the vendor's server every 15 seconds it's possible that all we'll be doing is exacerbating the problem. A more common approach when retrying failed tasks like network connections is to increase the delay exponentially. But there are a few considerations to keep in mind when doing this. It's important to keep the initial delay small and the number of retries low. If either number is too big then you'll end up with a script sleeping for hours waiting to retry a failed task, which probably isn't what you want either.

With those changes we end up with a thrifty way to retry the vendor transmission. We're leaving an audit trail of exceptions in a log file and exponentially backing off the retry:

```
retries = 0

begin
  service.update(record)
rescue VendorDeadlockError => e
  raise if retries >= 3
  retries += 1
  logger.warn("API failure: #{e}, retrying...")
  sleep(5 ** retries)
  retry
end
```

Things to Remember

+ Never use retry unconditionally; treat it like an implicit loop in your code. Create a variable outside the scope of a begin block and re-raise the exception if you've hit the upper bound on the retry limit.

+ Maintain an audit trail when using retry. If retrying problematic code doesn't go well you'll want to know the chain of events that led up to the final error.

+ When using a delay before a retry, consider increasing it within each rescue to avoid exacerbating the problem.

Item 27: Prefer throw to raise for Jumping Out of Scope

If you've ever painted yourself into a corner in Ruby you've probably turned to exceptions to jump up the stack. That is, you've used exceptions purely for control flow. This isn't uncommon, and in some situations it's even encouraged by Ruby:

```ruby
loop do
  answer = ui.prompt("command: ")
  raise(StopIteration) if answer == 'quit'
  ...
end
```

The loop method rescues the StopIteration exception as a signal to quit looping. This is mainly used for the interaction between loop and Enumerator#next so when running off the end of an enumerator it's able to terminate the outer loop. But you can see why it would be useful here too.

Another time you might lean toward exceptions for control flow is when you have nested loops or iterations and you want to break out of all of them at once. Ruby doesn't have loop labels like other languages, and if you try to use break, it will only terminate one of the loops. After being exposed to StopIteration it might be tempting to write something like this:

```ruby
begin
  @characters.each do |character|
    @colors.each do |color|
      if player.valid?(character, color)
        raise(StopIteration)
      end
    end
  end
rescue StopIteration
  ...
end
```

While there's nothing technically wrong with this approach, we have better tools at our disposal. Suppose you've written the code above that tries to find the first matching character/color combination. It would obviously be better if it communicated that information outside the nested loops. With the way things sit now we'd have to find a way to bury the matching character and color in the exception since that's the vehicle used to break out of the loops. Of course, refactoring so you could simply return the match would be ideal, but for this example let's take that option off the table.

Ruby has a control structure that is very similar to exceptions. You've probably come across it before and might even have been confused by the names of the keywords catch and throw. If you came to Ruby from C++ or Java these names can be confusing indeed. While not directly related to exceptions, this control structure acts in much the same way. You can almost think of catch and throw as safe versions of goto.

They work by labeling a section in your code with the catch keyword and then using throw to jump back to that label somewhere else. Like a propagating exception, when you use throw to jump across stack frames all the intermediate ensure clauses will run, making it safe to use this control structure.

```ruby
match = catch(:jump) do
  @characters.each do |character|
    @colors.each do |color|
      if player.valid?(character, color)
        throw(:jump, [character, color])
      end
    end
  end
end
```

As you can see, catch takes a symbol to use as the label and a block to execute. If throw is used in that block with the same label then catch will terminate the block and return the value given to throw. You don't have to pass a value to throw either; it's completely optional. If you omit the value it will be nil, or if throw isn't called during the execution of the block then catch will return the last value of its block. The only mandatory part of the throw invocation is the label symbol. If the throw label doesn't match the catch label the stack will unwind looking for a matching catch, eventually turning into a NameError exception if one can't be found.

The example above is nice because it's clear that catch and throw are connected to one another, mostly because they're in such close proximity. But that doesn't have to be the case. You can use throw to jump up the stack just like exceptions, so a call to throw can be several method calls away from catch. This might be useful, but it has the same drawbacks as exceptions. To understand code that uses throw or raise you need to think about the method calls as forming a call stack and start walking upward to see where the jump will stop.

Ideally, you should use the simplest control structure possible. If you find yourself using exceptions purely for control flow you might want to consider using catch and throw instead. But if you find yourself using catch and throw too often, you're probably doing something wrong.

Things to Remember

✦ Prefer using throw to raise when you need complicated control flow. An added bonus with throw is that you can send an object up the stack, which becomes the return value of catch.

✦ Use the simplest control structure possible. You can often rewrite a catch and throw combination as a pair of method calls that simply use return to jump out of scope.

 # Metaprogramming

In Ruby, everything is open to modification at run time. Classes, modules, and even the behavior of individual objects can all be changed while a program is running. It's trivial to write code that defines new classes or adds methods to an existing class or object. Virtually nothing is off limits. This so-called "metaprogramming" is one of Ruby's most powerful features. It's also one of its most dangerous.

There are a lot of good uses for metaprogramming. Cleaning up redundant code, generalizing a feature to work with more than one class, and creating domain-specific languages are just a few examples. But there are downsides, too. Methods like eval tend to become crutches, since they can be used to solve so many programming problems, yet at the same time they can expose your application to serious security issues. Knowing which kinds of metaprogramming are safe and helpful and which are problematic is the responsibility of every Ruby programmer.

Metaprogramming can be a slippery slope. This chapter will help you keep your footing.

Item 28: Familiarize Yourself with Module and Class Hooks

Love them or hate them, callbacks are a recurring pattern in software design. From user-interface event handling to asynchronous APIs, callbacks are practically everywhere. Working with a library or framework that requires callbacks isn't always the most enjoyable experience. That said, some languages make it more natural to pass functions or anonymous chunks of code around as callbacks. You could even consider a block in Ruby to be a type of callback. In that light, callbacks don't seem so bad after all.

At the risk of outing myself, my favorite text editor uses callbacks as a way to hook into nearly every feature it offers. I love them. I can write a so-called hook function to be notified before or after a file has been opened, saved, or closed. Almost every action performed in my editor triggers an event that runs registered hook functions. I've done some pretty weird stuff using hooks, but always for the greater good, of course.

Ruby also uses this idea of events and hook functions, although a much simpler model. Registering to receive event notifications is as simple as writing a method with the correct name. No doubt you've already done something similar by defining methods such as `initialize` and `method_missing`. While these methods do seem to be callbacks with respect to object lifetimes and method dispatching, Ruby doesn't consider them hooks. Technically, hooks facilitate metaprogramming at the class and module level and are therefore written as class and module methods (also known as singleton methods). There are about a dozen such methods you can define, but let's start with the most frequently used hooks.

As you know, it's quite common to mix modules into objects, classes, and other modules using the `include` and `extend` methods. Each time you mix in a module Ruby calls the `included` or `extended` hook depending on how the module was mixed in. This is basically a notification to the module that it's being inserted into a class hierarchy somewhere. Both hooks are given a single argument: the receiver of the `include` or `extend` method. In other words, the argument is the object doing the including or extending. What can you do with one of these hooks? Let's explore the `extended` hook by revisiting the example from Item 21.

Recall that the `RaisingHash` class used delegation instead of inheritance to reuse the functionality of the `Hash` class. The major difference between `Hash` and `RaisingHash` is that the latter raises an exception if a nonexistent key is accessed. The majority of the `Hash` instance methods were made available as instance methods in `RaisingHash` using the `def_delegators` method from the `Forwardable` module. These delegated methods in `RaisingHash` simply forward the method call on to the `@hash` instance variable.

But there were a few instance methods that weren't so simple. The `freeze`, `taint`, and `untaint` methods needed to invoke the appropriate method on `@hash`, followed by a call to `super`, so the `RaisingHash` object itself was updated accordingly. The implementations of these methods were almost identical. Let's fix that by writing a new delegation helper method that calls `super` after delegating the method to `@hash`. Now, we could just add this new method to the existing `Forwardable` module, but Item 32 advises against this. Instead, let's write a new module called `SuperForwardable`. To make life a bit easier for users of `SuperForwardable`, we'll use the `extended` module hook to make sure the `Forwardable` library file is loaded and any class that extends `SuperForwardable` also extends `Forwardable`. Consider this:

```ruby
module SuperForwardable

  # Module hook.

  def self.extended (klass)
    require('forwardable')
    klass.extend(Forwardable)
  end

  # Creates delegator which calls super.

  def def_delegators_with_super (target, *methods)
    methods.each do |method|
      target_method = "#{method}_without_super".to_sym
      def_delegator(target, method, target_method)

      define_method(method) do |*args, &block|
        send(target_method, *args, &block)
        super(*args, &block)
      end
    end
  end
end
```

Extending a class with the SuperForwardable module triggers the
SuperForwardable::extended hook method. This method is given the
object doing the extending as its only argument. It's common practice to name this argument klass or mod, depending on how you
assume the module is going to be used. The name "klass" is used
because "class" is a keyword in Ruby and can't be used as a variable
name. The extended hook in SuperForwardable expects to be given a
class that it then extends with the Forwardable module. So extending
a class with SuperForwardable not only brings in all of the methods
defined in that module, it also brings in all of the methods defined in
the Forwardable module. Let's see how we can use this new module
from within the RaisingHash class:

```ruby
class RaisingHash
  extend(SuperForwardable)
  def_delegators(:@hash, :[], :[]=) # etc.
  def_delegators_with_super(:@hash, :freeze, :taint, :untaint)

  def initialize
    # Create @hash...
  end
end
```

Okay, let's take a moment and trace what's going on in the RaisingHash class definition. The first line in the class uses the extend method with a single argument: the SuperForwardable module. The extend method can actually take any number of modules as arguments. For each module the extend method adds all of the methods and constants defined in the module to the receiver. For the RaisingHash class this means that the single instance method defined in SuperForwardable becomes a class method in RaisingHash.

After all of the definitions from the module are loaded into the receiver, extend invokes the module's extended hook. When the hook method is called it is passed the object that invoked extend. In our example, SuperForwardable::extended is called with RaisingHash as its argument. This leads to SuperForwardable::extended calling RaisingHash::extend and passing in the Forwardable module. This whole process repeats so that the Forwardable module is loaded into RaisingHash.

With SuperForwardable and Forwardable loaded into RaisingHash we can use def_delegators and def_delegators_with_super to set up the method forwarding to @hash. We've seen def_delegators before in Item 21, and def_delegators_with_super does the exact same thing, with one exception. After forwarding the original method call to the target object, the generated delegation method also calls super. Using this helper method gives RaisingHash three new instance methods: freeze, taint, and untaint. Each method calls a corresponding method on the @hash object followed by super.

Using the extended hook in a module to further extend a class is an interesting way to emulate module inheritance. It's as if the SuperForwardable module inherited from the Forwardable module. A similar sort of thing can be done with the include method and the included hook. Of course, the include method brings in a module's instance methods and sets them up as instance methods on the receiver. Mixing in a module with the include method triggers the included hook, which is defined just like the extended hook was in SuperForwardable.

The extended and included hooks are unique to modules. There's also a third hook that was introduced in Ruby 2.0: prepended. It's triggered when you use the prepend method to mix in a module. The prepended hook and the prepend method are discussed further in Item 35.

Almost all of the remaining hooks are available on modules *and* classes. The one exception is unique because it only works with classes. Each time a class is defined, Ruby triggers the inherited hook on its parent class to notify it about the new subclass. Let's do something interesting with this hook. Item 21 makes the case that you should never inherit from the core collection classes. Let's enforce that with some code.

We can use the inherited hook to intercept a class definition and raise an exception, preventing the inheritance. Since we want this logic to apply to all of the core collection classes, it makes sense to write it into a module. We can then use extend to insert the module's instance methods as class methods on each of the core collection classes. Consider the PreventInheritance module:

```
module PreventInheritance
  class InheritanceError < StandardError; end

  def inherited (child)
    raise(InheritanceError,
        "#{child} cannot inherit from #{self}")
  end
end
```

As an instance method in a module, the inherited method does nothing special. But turn it into a class method using extend and it becomes a proper hook method:

```
irb> Array.extend(PreventInheritance)

irb> class BetterArray < Array; end
PreventInheritance::InheritanceError:
    BetterArray cannot inherit from Array
```

Defining a hook in a module and then mixing it into a class is rather indirect, but useful in this case. If you want to define an inherited hook directly in a class you need to make sure it's a class method. For example:

```
class Parent
  def self.inherited (child)
    ...
  end
end
```

The Parent::inherited method will be called anytime a class is defined that inherits from the Parent class. It's worth mentioning that when the inherited hook is called, the child class isn't fully defined. That is, the body of the child class hasn't yet executed and so hasn't had a chance to define any methods. This may limit what you can do in an inherited hook, which is something you'll want to keep in mind.

That leaves us with the final six hooks that apply to both modules and classes alike. All of them have to do with methods. The method_added,

method_removed, and method_undefined hooks are for instance methods, while the singleton_method_added, singleton_method_removed, and
singleton_method_undefined hooks are for class and module methods.

Defining these hooks for modules or classes is similar to the previous
hooks we've seen. All of them should be defined in modules as module methods and in classes as class methods. Here's an example of a
class that monitors instance methods:

```ruby
class InstanceMethodWatcher
  def self.method_added     (m); end
  def self.method_removed   (m); end
  def self.method_undefined (m); end

  # Triggers method_added(:hello)
  def hello; end

  # Triggers method_removed(:hello)
  remove_method(:hello)

  # Triggers method_added(:hello), again.
  def hello; end

  # Triggers method_undefined(:hello)
  undef_method(:hello)
end
```

There are a couple of things to watch out for when using these hooks.
The only argument that is given to each of the hooks is a symbol representing the name of the method that was added, removed, or undefined. You're not given the class for which the method status changed.
If a method is added to a subclass, you'll need to rely on the value of
self to know that. Speaking of subclasses, since classes can partici-
pate in inheritance, you should probably call super from within these
hooks. See Item 29 for more information on hooks and super (including the inherited hook).

Hooks relating to singleton methods are very similar to their instance-
method counterparts, except for one strange side effect. Defining a
singleton_method_added hook will trigger itself. That is, defining
the hook—which is a singleton method—causes Ruby to trigger the
singleton_method_added hook that now exists. You'll want to watch
out for that. Otherwise, just remember that class methods are implemented as singleton methods, which is why the following code uses
the "class << self" trick to enter into the singleton class before invoking remove_method or undef_method:

```ruby
class SingletonMethodWatcher
  def self.singleton_method_added     (m); end
  def self.singleton_method_removed   (m); end
  def self.singleton_method_undefined (m); end

  # Triggers singleton_method_added(:hello)
  def self.hello; end

  # Triggers singleton_method_removed(:hello)
  class << self; remove_method(:hello); end

  # Triggers singleton_method_added(:hello), again.
  def self.hello; end

  # Triggers singleton_method_undefined(:hello)
  class << self; undef_method(:hello); end
end
```

And there you have it...all ten hook methods. Let's wrap up with a few notes about hooks. First, all the hook methods are automatically marked as private. They're meant to be called by the Ruby interpreter and not from user space for obvious reasons. Second, there are three methods that are related to the hook methods but are not hooks themselves: extend_object, append_features, and prepend_features.

None of these methods should be overridden. After all, that's what the hooks are for. As an example, when you use the include method to mix a module into a class, the module's append_features method is invoked to do the actual work before the included hook is triggered. While you could certainly override the append_features method and call super, the preferred way of intercepting this type of module mixing is by defining the included hook. The same thing goes for extend_object and the extended hook and prepend_features and the prepended hook. Prefer defining hook methods to overriding these internal methods.

Things to Remember

♦ All of the hook methods should be defined as singleton methods.

♦ The hooks that are called when a method is added, removed, or undefined only receive the name of the method, not the class where the change occurred. Use the value of self if you need to know this.

♦ Defining a singleton_method_added hook will trigger itself.

♦ Don't override the extend_object, append_features, or prepend_features methods. Use the extended, included, or prepended hooks instead.

Item 29: Invoke super from within Class Hooks

Let's say that after reading Item 28 you became really excited about using hook functions, specifically the `inherited` class hook. As a matter of fact, it solves a problem you've been having with one of your class hierarchies. Suppose that the base class of the troublesome hierarchy uses the factory method pattern. It's an abstract class representing an interface for downloading files when given URLs. Each subclass knows how to work with a single protocol such as HTTP or FTP. The application you're writing only has to pass a URL to the base class, and in response, it receives back an instance of the appropriate subclass ready to download the specified file.

The problem you've been having has to do with the base class knowing about each of its subclasses. Up to this point, you've had to manually connect everything together. But now, with the `inherited` hook, things are much easier. Consider this:

```ruby
class DownloaderBase
  def self.inherited (subclass)
    handlers << subclass
  end

  def self.handlers
    @handlers ||= []
  end

  private_class_method(:handlers)
end
```

Thanks to the `inherited` hook, the subclasses will now automatically register themselves with the base class when they are defined. As recommended in Item 15, the base class uses a class-instance variable to track all of its subclasses as opposed to a regular class variable. This keeps it from appearing in the subclasses and avoids any accidental mutation.

With just a few more methods the `DownloaderBase` class will be able to accept a URL and return the appropriate subclass. But there's something missing in the `inherited` hook that's more important for our discussion here, it needs to invoke super. Technically, the `inherited` hook works fine just the way it is. The `DownloaderBase` implicitly inherits from `Object` so there's no real need to use super to call an `inherited` hook higher up in the hierarchy. But as we've seen before, inheritance isn't the only way for a class to be associated with a superclass.

Including or extending a module might insert an `inherited` hook higher in the hierarchy. Popular frameworks such as Ruby on Rails do this from time to time. Take the ActiveModel::Validations module, for example. When you include that module into a class it sets up an inherited hook that copies any attribute validation callbacks into subclasses. If you tried to use the ActiveModel::Validations module with the current implementation of DownloaderBase, this copying wouldn't happen. Other modules with more important inherited hooks might break entirely. Of course, the solution is simple—make sure you call super:

```
def self.inherited (subclass)
  super
  handlers << subclass
end
```

As the title of this item suggests, this advice goes beyond the inherited hook. All of the class hooks should invoke versions of themselves higher up in the hierarchy using super. (For a full list of class hooks go back and take a look at Item 28.)

It might seem redundant to use super from hooks in classes like DownloaderBase, and perhaps it is. Keep in mind that since modules can insert class hooks, it's not always obvious when the hook you're writing might override another one higher up in the inheritance hierarchy. Using super is good way to future-proof your code, but ultimately, you'll have to use your best judgment.

Things to Remember

✦ Invoke super from within class hooks.

Item 30: Prefer define_method to method_missing

When newcomers to Ruby discover method_missing, it's as if they've just found a multipurpose tool that is begging to be used. It calls to them while in the shower and professes itself to be the perfect solution to a difficult problem from the previous day. One way or another, method_missing is going to end up in their code, even if they have to use a crowbar to get it to fit. What is it about method_missing that makes it so attractive?

Clearly, method_missing is one of the most powerful tools in the Ruby toolbox. Unfortunately, it has a lot of dubious uses. Want an object to respond to any possible message? No problem. Ever needed a Hash to act more like an OpenStruct? Piece of cake. Do you like the idea of method names automatically being turned into SQL? Take a look at Rails 2. It only goes downhill from there.

You can do all these things with method_missing because it's a catch-all, your last ditch effort to respond to a message when a matching method can't be found. But it comes with a cost. We've already seen in Item 7 how defining method_missing can lead to confusing error messages when using super. Then you have introspection methods like respond_to? that don't agree with reality. There's also a small performance difference when you use method_missing due to the extra traversal of the inheritance hierarchy, but it's fairly negligible so we won't consider it further.

The good news is that there's nearly always a way to implement the same features without resorting to method_missing. In order to demonstrate this I'll tackle two of the most common uses of method_missing and show how define_method can be used without incurring the drawbacks listed above. Let's start with the biggest use of method_missing: proxies.

We've already seen how to use the Forwardable module to delegate methods to an instance variable. Back in Item 21 we looked at the RaisingHash class that forwarded many of its instance methods without ever exposing the internal hash kept in @hash. This is a great use of the Forwardable module and the way I recommend you implement delegators or proxies. Unfortunately, the Forwardable module isn't well known and method_missing *seems* to be the next best thing. Consider the HashProxy class:

```ruby
class HashProxy
  def initialize
    @hash = {}
  end

  private

  def method_missing (name, *args, &block)
    if @hash.respond_to?(name)
      @hash.send(name, *args, &block)
    else
      super
    end
  end
end
```

This very simple class uses method_missing to forward all undefined methods to its @hash instance variable. That is, as long as the hash object responds to the current message. If it doesn't, method_missing calls super so that the version of method_missing in the BasicObject class can raise a NoMethodError exception. My biggest complaint about this class is that while it's pretending to be a Hash, it doesn't do a very good job. Consider this:

```
irb> h = HashProxy.new

irb> h.respond_to?(:size)
---> false

irb> h.size
---> 0

irb> h.public_methods(false)
---> []
```

Ruby programmers espouse that duck typing is the correct way to work with dynamic types. The type of an object isn't what's important; it's the interface that you should be concerned with. But using method_missing this way exposes no interface at all. Using respond_to? and other introspective methods to confirm that an object supports the needed interface isn't possible. Even if you prefer run-time NoMethodError exceptions to using respond_to?, there's no good reason why delegation can't be implemented properly. (One way to fix respond_to? is with respond_to_missing?. We'll look at why it's not a great solution in just a bit.)

If you've decided that the Forwardable module won't work for you, the next best thing is to use define_method. That's essentially what the Forwardable module is doing behind the scenes anyway. Given a method name and a block, define_method will create an instance method whose body and arguments are specified by the block. It's a private class method so you can't call it with a receiver. But that's usually not a problem. Consider this implementation of the HashProxy class:

```
class HashProxy
  Hash.public_instance_methods(false).each do |name|
    define_method(name) do |*args, &block|
      @hash.send(name, *args, &block)
    end
  end

  def initialize
    @hash = {}
  end
end
```

This version uses a little metaprogramming to iterate over the public instance methods from the Hash class. For each of them, an instance method is created in HashProxy using define_method. The generated methods simply forward their messages on to the @hash object. The effect is the same as the version that used `method_missing`, but this implementation is more explicit and correctly exposes a Hash-like interface. See for yourself:

```
irb> h = HashProxy.new

irb> h.respond_to?(:size)
---> true

irb> h.public_methods(false).sort.take(5)
---> [:==, :[], :[]=, :assoc, :clear]
```

Ah...that looks much better. I would argue that using `define_method` in this case isn't any more complicated than using `method_missing`. In fact, I'd say that it's quite a bit clearer and you don't have to guess what's going on. It's too easy for `method_missing` to become a black hole of confusion. Hopefully, you can now see that it's also easy to replace it with `define_method`. Let's solidify this by looking at a more complicated example.

The next major thing Ruby programmers use `method_missing` for is to implement the decorator pattern. This pattern is very similar to the delegation pattern we just explored, but with a twist. Classes implementing the decorator pattern wrap an arbitrary object and extend its capabilities in some way. In the `HashProxy` class we knew ahead of time that we'd be forwarding messages to a hash object. The decorator class, on the other hand, accepts objects of any class and needs to delegate to them appropriately. Let's write a decorator class that records log entries before delegating to the target object. It's pretty easy to implement using `method_missing`:

```
class AuditDecorator
  def initialize (object)
    @object = object
    @logger = Logger.new($stdout)
  end

  private

  def method_missing (name, *args, &block)
    @logger.info("calling '#{name}' on #{@object.inspect}")
    @object.send(name, *args, &block)
  end
end
```

The `AuditDecorator` class can add a method-logging feature to any object. Calling a method on an instance of `AuditDecorator` will log the message and then forward it to the wrapped object, with an exception, of course. Methods already defined in AuditDecorator (or its super-classes) won't trigger method_missing. So, implementing the decorator pattern this way isn't as transparent as we'd like. Consider this:

```
irb> fake = AuditDecorator.new("Am I a String?")

irb> fake.downcase
INFO: calling 'downcase' on "Am I a String?"
---> "am i a string?"

irb> fake.class
---> AuditDecorator
```

As before, using method_missing means that AuditDecorator instances don't respond correctly to introspective methods such as respond_to? and public_methods. But now we have an additional problem. The AuditDecorator instance methods get in the way and keep us from logging and forwarding methods like class. Ideally, the decorator class would be completely transparent and would forward *all* methods. That's where define_method comes in. However, since the AuditDecorator class can wrap any object we're going to have to rely on a little more metaprogramming to make this work. The initialize method needs to inspect the object it's wrapping and then create the appropriate forwarding methods. But those methods can't be instance methods for the AuditDecorator class, since each instance should be able to wrap different objects with different classes. So, the generated methods will have to exist in a single instance of AuditDecorator and not for all AuditDecorator instances. Thankfully, we have anonymous modules to work with:

```ruby
class AuditDecorator
  def initialize (object)
    @object = object
    @logger = Logger.new($stdout)

    mod = Module.new do
      object.public_methods.each do |name|
        define_method(name) do |*args, &block|
          @logger.info("calling '#{name}' on #{@object.inspect}")
          @object.send(name, *args, &block)
        end
      end
    end

    extend(mod)
  end
end
```

There's a bit more going on in this version than with its predecessor. To generate methods on the current AuditDecorator instance (as opposed to all AuditDecorator instances) we need to create an anonymous module and define the methods we want *inside* the module. Then, all we have to do is extend the AuditDecorator instance with the anonymous module, thus copying all of those generated methods into the instance. Pretty slick, huh? In exchange for a few extra lines of code we now have full transparency:

```
irb> fake = AuditDecorator.new("I'm a String!")

irb> fake.downcase
INFO: calling 'downcase' on "I'm a String!"
---> "i'm a string!"

irb> fake.class
INFO: calling 'class' on "I'm a String!"
---> String
```

But there's one very subtle but important point you need to consider here. Did you notice that inside the block given to Module::new the public_methods message was sent to the object variable and not @object? That's because inside the module—but outside a method definition—@object refers to a module variable and not the instance variable defined in AuditDecorator#initialize. But the block does form a closure that allows us to access the local variables defined in the initialize method. That's why using the object variable works from inside the module. Knowing about these scoping rules will keep you from pulling your hair out while you're exercising Ruby's metaprogramming features.

I would be remiss if I didn't mention a method related to define_method. While only modules and classes respond to define_method, objects have their own version called define_singleton_method. Thanks to this metaprogramming gem we can remove the need for Module::new in the previous example. Using define_singleton_method has the same effect as defining a method in an anonymous module that is then extended:

```
class AuditDecorator
  def initialize (object)
    @object = object
    @logger = Logger.new($stdout)

    @object.public_methods.each do |name|
      define_singleton_method(name) do |*args, &block|
```

```
            @logger.info("calling '#{name}' on #{@object.inspect}")
            @object.send(name, *args, &block)
        end
      end
    end
  end
```

Replacing method_missing with define_method doesn't just make your code more explicit, it also restores proper introspection capabilities, and in the case of the decorator pattern, allows for complete transparency. Before reaching for method_missing you should consider whether using defined_method is possible. I've yet to find a situation where method_missing was the only possible solution. If you do find yourself unable to use defined_method (or define_singleton_method), there's one last trick you should know about.

Just as method_missing is a catchall for method dispatch, introspection in Ruby uses the respond_to_missing? method as a half-baked callback. If you define this method it will be called for two different reasons. First, if you use respond_to? to see if an object responds to a specific message and a matching method isn't defined, respond_to? will invoke respond_to_missing?, giving you the opportunity to make respond_to? return true. For the HashProxy above you'd want to implement the respond_to_missing? method like this:

```
def respond_to_missing? (name, include_private)
  @hash.respond_to?(name, include_private) || super
end
```

Adding this code to the HashProxy class would allow the respond_to? method to return true for all of the Hash instance methods. The reason I said that it's half-baked is because it doesn't have any effect on methods like public_methods. This leads to some of the introspective methods reporting that a method exists, while others say it doesn't. In my opinion, that's even more confusing. If you're using method_missing it's the best you can do.

The other reason respond_to_missing? is used has to do with an interesting method that goes by the name "method". It takes the name of a method and returns an object that can be used to invoke the method at a later time. If you call method for a method that isn't defined but for which respond_to_missing? returns true, Ruby will return a Method object that encapsulates a call to method_missing. Again, this is another example where some methods report one interface and other methods report a different interface (something that isn't a problem with define_method).

Things to Remember

✦ Prefer define_method to method_missing.

✦ If you absolutely must use method_missing consider defining respond_to_missing?.

Item 31: Know the Difference between the Variants of eval

We've seen that Ruby has a rich set of features for run-time metaprogramming, and without a doubt, the most powerful of these are the family of eval methods. The vanilla eval method is similar to those found in other interpreted languages—you build up a string of valid Ruby code and have it evaluated at run time. Of course, this can be very dangerous, especially in an application that is processing untrustworthy data. Fortunately, there's rarely ever a valid reason to evaluate a string these days. That's because the majority of the evaluation methods in Ruby all except blocks of code. Combined with metaprogramming tricks like define_method, you can replace nearly every use of string evaluation with block evaluation. Throughout this item you'll see just how easy it is to rid yourself of string evaluation and replace it with something safer and more sensible.

You've probably already seen several methods in Ruby with the word "eval" in their name. There are a lot of evaluation methods and knowing which of them to use for a particular task can be confusing. Most of them have names that hint at how they work— or more accurately, the context in which they evaluate their input. That's the major differentiating feature between them, that and what they're willing to evaluate: strings, blocks, or both. Most of the evaluation methods use their receiver as the evaluation context. A notable exception is the eval method from the Kernel module.

While eval only accepts strings as input, you can have that string evaluated in any context you want. If you don't specify a context, the string is evaluated as if it were written into the code at the point where eval is used, and that's not always desirable. Perhaps you don't want to expose the variables that are currently in scope. In this case, you can explicitly provide a Binding object that represents the context in which the string should be evaluated. The Kernel module defines a private method named binding that captures the local scope and returns it inside a Binding object. This context can then be given to eval as its second argument:

```
irb> def glass_case_of_emotion
        x = "I'm in a " + __method__.to_s.tr('_', ' ')
        binding
     end

irb> x = "I'm in scope"

irb> eval("x")
---> "I'm in scope"

irb> eval("x", glass_case_of_emotion)
---> "I'm in a glass case of emotion"
```

Being able to specify the exact context to use for evaluation is pretty neat. But eval only accepts strings as input, so you need to be very careful about what goes into them. Allowing any untrustworthy data (such as user input) to make their way into eval exposes your application to code injection attacks. That's why we'll turn our attention away from strings and toward blocks. All of the remaining evaluation methods support blocks as input. The only difference between them is the context they use when evaluating those blocks.

Thanks to the BasicObject class, every object in Ruby responds to the instance_eval method. Its name provides a clue about the context it uses when evaluating its input. Unlike with eval, you can't provide a Binding object directly to instance_eval. Instead, the object you invoke instance_eval on becomes the context for the evaluation. This allows you to reach into an object and access its private methods and instance variables. Things get a little confusing when you start defining methods with instance_eval. Let's play around with the evaluation methods and look at a simple Widget class:

```
class Widget
  def initialize (name)
    @name = name
  end
end
```

Using this class we can see how instance_eval can be used to access instance variables and define methods:

```
irb> w = Widget.new("Muffler Bearing")

irb> w.instance_eval {@name}
---> "Muffler Bearing"

irb> w.instance_eval do
```

```
        def in_stock?; false; end
      end
```

```
irb> w.singleton_methods(false)
---> [:in_stock?]
```

If you use instance_eval to define a method that method will only
exist for a single object. In other words, instance_eval creates singleton methods. What happens if you use instance_eval with a class
object? What are singleton methods in the context of a class? Yep,
class methods. Observe:

```
irb> Widget.instance_eval do
        def table_name; "widgets"; end
      end
```

```
irb> Widget.table_name
---> "widgets"
```

```
irb> Widget.singleton_methods(false)
---> [:table_name]
```

It might be a bit confusing at first, but if you remember that methods
defined using instance_eval are singleton methods, you'll be in good
shape. On the other hand, what if we wanted to define an instance
method in the Widget class so that it's available to all instances? That's
where our next evaluation method comes in: class_eval. Just as its
name suggests, class_eval evaluates a string or a block in the context
of a class. It's exactly like opening the class back up and inserting new
code. Anything you can do between the class and end keywords in a
normal class definition can be done using class_eval. For example:

```
irb> Widget.class_eval do
        attr_accessor(:name)
        def sold?; false; end
      end
```

```
irb> w = Widget.new("Blinker Fluid")
```

```
irb> w.public_methods(false)
---> [:name, :name=, :sold?]
```

But you can't use class_eval on just any object. As a matter of fact,
it's defined in the Module class as a singleton method, which means it
can only be used on modules and classes. There's even an alias for it
so you can make your code look better when you're manipulating
modules: module_eval. But it's purely aesthetics—there's no difference
between class_eval and module_eval.

An easy way to remember the context for these evaluation methods is to think about the receiver. While evaluating their input the instance_eval and class_eval methods set the self variable to their receiver. That's why you can access instance variables with instance_eval and define instance methods with class_eval. They also yield their receiver to the input block. Sometimes this can be useful if there's some indirection between the receiver and the block. For example, consider this variant of the Widget class:

```
class Widget
  attr_accessor(:name, :quantity)

  def initialize (&block)
    instance_eval(&block) if block
  end
end
irb> w = Widget.new do |widget|
       widget.name = "Elbow Grease"
       @quantity = 0
     end

irb> [w.name, w.quantity]
---> ["Elbow Grease", 0]
```

Because the block given to initialize is passed to instance_eval, it is evaluated in the context of the new Widget object. When instance_eval invokes the block it sets self to its receiver (the Widget object) and yields the same object to the block. Since the self variable is set to the Widget object the block can manipulate internal instance variables directly as if it were an instance method. This might sometimes be useful, but it does break encapsulation.

So far we've focused on some simple uses of run-time evaluation. It might seem like evaluating a block isn't as flexible as evaluating a string since you're stuck with static code. This is reinforced by the fact that it's quite common to see instance_eval or class_eval used in Ruby libraries out in the wild with strings instead of blocks. Let's put this myth to bed using the final set of evaluation methods: instance_exec, class_exec, and module_exec.

These methods are very similar to their eval counterparts. Where the eval versions accept strings *or* blocks the exec variants only accept blocks. They also differ in what they yield to their blocks. The exec methods don't yield anything to their blocks by default. Instead, any arguments given to them are passed on to the block. This gives us enough power to do just about everything we can do when evaluating strings.

Suppose you have a class to represent a counter that can be used to increment an instance variable, but not reset it back to its starting value. Why can't you reset it? Don't ask me...this is supposed to be your code, not mine. Also suppose that you don't want to add a reset feature directly to the class, but instead want to reset counter objects externally. Consider this:

```
class Counter
  DEFAULT = 0
  attr_reader(:counter)

  def initialize (start=DEFAULT)
    @counter = start
  end

  def inc
    @counter += 1
  end
end
```

You'd like to reset the @counter instance variable back to the value set in the DEFAULT constant. You also want to make this code generic so you can use it with other classes in the future. As a first stab in the dark you resort to evaluating a string:

```
module Reset
  def self.reset_var (object, name)
    object.instance_eval("@#{name} = DEFAULT")
  end
end
```

Using this helper method is pretty straightforward. If you give the reset_var module function an object and a variable name it will set an instance variable with that name to the value in DEFAULT. But notice what happens if you give it an invalid variable name:

```
irb> c = Counter.new(10)
---> #<Counter @counter=10>

irb> Reset.reset_var(c, "counter")
---> 0

irb> Reset.reset_var(c, "x;")
SyntaxError: (eval):1:
    syntax error, unexpected '=', expecting end-of-input
```

This example might be slightly contrived, but it does demonstrate how to inject code into an evaluation method. Let's look at how we can use instance_exec to write reset_var without having to evaluate a string. Since instance_exec will pass its arguments on to the block that it evaluates, we can use that as a way to pass constructed names into the block for use in methods like instance_variable_set:

```
module Reset
  def self.reset_var (object, name)
    object.instance_exec("@#{name}".to_sym) do |var|
      const = self.class.const_get(:DEFAULT)
      instance_variable_set(var, const)
    end
  end
end
```

Ruby's metaprogramming API is rich enough that we rarely need to even use the evaluation methods, especially those that evaluate strings. Methods like define_method and instance_variable_set are also much easier to read than a mess of strings with interpolated variables. Back to our use of instance_exec, look at what happens now if you give reset_var a bad variable name:

```
irb> Reset.reset_var(c, "x;")
NameError: '@x;' is not allowed as an instance variable name
```

This time the code raises a NameError, unlike the previous version, which raised a SyntaxError. Of course, the difference is that the string that was passed to reset_var wasn't evaluated as Ruby code. Instead, it was only used to look up an instance variable in an object's variable table. But before that even happened it was validated to ensure that it could be used as a valid variable name, which failed and raised an exception. This is another important difference between the variants of eval, one you'll want to keep in mind.

Things to Remember

+ Methods defined using instance_eval or instance_exec are singleton methods.

+ The class_eval, module_eval, class_exec, and module_exec methods can only be used with classes and modules. Methods defined with one of these become instance methods.

Item 32: Consider Alternatives to Monkey Patching

Unless you've been living on an island where this book happened to wash up you've no doubt heard of Ruby on Rails. It made a pretty big splash in the web-application development community and helped put Ruby in the spotlight. But it hasn't been all rainbows and roses. Rails includes a library called Active Support, which modifies nearly every Ruby core class, something referred to as "monkey patching."

While it's not a new concept, Active Support's heavy use of monkey patching kicked up quite a bit of dust in the Ruby community. The lines were drawn—you were either for or against monkey patching. Okay, maybe it wasn't that dramatic, but there are definitely some outspoken Ruby experts who strongly advise against modifying the core classes. So, what's the harm? What's so bad about monkey patching?

As you know, classes, objects, and modules are always open in Ruby. You can modify them at any point while a program is running. Nothing is really off limits. Maybe you'll get a run-time warning, maybe not. Have you ever wished that the String class had a to_french method? No problem—open the class or use something like class_exec to add it. But what if one of the libraries you're using in a project also adds a String#to_french method? This is a pretty big problem and is often referred to as patch collision. Ruby will definitely give you a warning if you redefine an existing method, which is why Item 5 urges you to pay attention to run-time warnings. But as we'll see shortly, there are ways to run into patch collision *without* triggering a warning.

Now, if both of the colliding methods do the exact same thing, maybe you won't care as much. If they happen to do completely different things but collide because they have the same name, well, you'll probably care a lot more. Actually, both situations seem pretty serious to me. I want to know for sure which implementation of a method I'm using and that it's been tested appropriately. Imagine tearing your hair out because your code looks totally fine, except thanks to monkey patching, it's not your code that is actually running and breaking things. Trust me...this has happened to me more than once. Clearly, monkey patching can be dangerous. That's why we're going to explore alternatives, ways to do some of the same things you can do with monkey patching but with different trade-offs.

There are a handful of RubyGems (including Active Support) that monkey patch the String class to add a method that tests if a string is empty or only includes space characters. It's a surprisingly useful feature that has somehow avoided getting included into the official String class. Let's write our own version of this method and experiment with a few ways to use it without resorting to altering the String class. One of the safest ways to write this method is to make it a module function. Consider this:

```ruby
module OnlySpace
  ONLY_SPACE_UNICODE_RE = %r/\A[[:space:]]*\z/

  def self.only_space? (str)
    if str.ascii_only?
      !str.bytes.any? {|b| b != 32 && !b.between?(9, 13)}
    else
      ONLY_SPACE_UNICODE_RE === str
    end
  end
end
```

The only_space? method is callable directly through the OnlySpace module. The biggest downsides to this technique are rather obvious. It's not very object-oriented and it's a bit verbose. Using the module function is simple, but just doesn't feel right:

```ruby
irb> OnlySpace.only_space?("\r\n")
---> true
```

One way to improve upon this is to define an instance method version of only_space? in the OnlySpace module. You can then extend individual string objects as necessary.

```ruby
module OnlySpace
  def only_space?
    # Forward to module function.
    OnlySpace.only_space?(self)
  end
end
irb> str = "Yo Ho!"

irb> str.extend(OnlySpace)

irb> str.only_space?
---> false
```

While this restores some object-oriented flavoring, it's still a bit long-winded. The upside is that we've managed to avoid monkey patching the String class. Strings that haven't been extended by our module won't be affected. On the other hand, this technique introduces inconsistency because some string objects will respond to only_space?, while others won't. Extending individual objects with a module tends to work best when very little of your code needs to use the methods defined in that module. As you use those methods more often, you'll probably want to consider another alternative.

Even though extending individual string objects with the OnlySpace module doesn't alter the String class in any way, it is still a form of monkey patching, albeit on a smaller scale and a bit more controlled. To completely avoid monkey patching altogether, let's turn to our next technique—creating a new String class.

Back in Item 21 we looked at changing the behavior of the Hash class by writing a new class, RaisingHash. We avoided inheritance in order to maintain total control over which methods were exposed by the RaisingHash class. Instead, RaisingHash stored a hash inside an instance variable. It then used method delegation to forward methods to the hash using the Forwardable module. We can use this technique to create a new string class:

```ruby
require('forwardable')

class StringExtra
  extend(Forwardable)
  def_delegators(:@string,
                 *String.public_instance_methods(false))

  def initialize (str="")
    @string = str
  end

  def only_space?
    ...
  end
end
```

The StringExtra class works just like the core String class thanks to the Forwardable module and the def_delegators method. Unlike with the RaisingHash class, I haven't overridden any methods that might return a new String object instead of a StringExtra object. I also haven't implemented some important methods like freeze and taint. If you define a delegating class like StringExtra, make sure you go back to Item 21 and add these missing features.

Using StringExtra::new to wrap an existing string object can be easier to stomach than using the extend method. Both techniques suffer from the fact that you need to take an extra step to get an object that responds to the only_space? message. The String class has a monopoly on automatic string creation from syntax literals. There's just no getting away from needing to take this extra step if you want to avoid monkey patching. Then again, if you tuck the call to StringExtra::new away in your initialize method, it's not such a big deal. And it's a lot less painful than having to debug the mess caused by adding methods to an existing class.

But sometimes, even after considering the alternatives, you still want to modify one of the core classes. If you're using at least Ruby 2.0, there's a feature specifically designed to rein in monkey patching: It's called refinements. You can think of refinements as being somewhat similar to the StringExtra class, except that Ruby will automatically wrap and unwrap the string that we want to add extra features to. There are two parts to refinements: modifying a class in some way (usually by adding instance methods) and activating those changes with a limited visibility (using lexical scopes).

Refinements are a very interesting way to deal with monkey patching, but they do come with some limitations. The biggest limitation may be that refinements are relatively new to Ruby and they're still in flux. As I mentioned earlier, they were introduced in Ruby 2.0 as an experimental feature. Defining and activating refinements will produce run-time warnings reminding you that these features are subject to change. Starting in Ruby 2.1 refinements are no longer an experimental feature and won't produce any warnings. But the feature still isn't considered stable and the next version of Ruby might change refinements as necessary.

Another limitation is that you can only refine classes. Attempting to refine anything else—like a module—will raise a TypeError exception. While this probably isn't too restrictive, it's something to keep in mind.

Defining a refinement is done inside a module using the refine method. You pass in the class you plan to modify as the argument to refine and do any necessary patching inside a block. Take a look at a refinement that adds the only_space? method to String:

```ruby
module OnlySpace
  refine(String) do
    def only_space?
      ...
    end
  end
end
```

Using the refine method to define a refinement isn't enough to add the only_space? method to String, it's just the first step. The next thing you need to do is to activate the refinement with the using method. This is where things get a little tricky. Ruby 2.0 only allows you to activate a refinement at the top level of a file, outside of any module or class definition. After activating the refinement it will be available from that point until the end of the file. Ruby 2.1 is more flexible. You can activate a refinement at the top level of a file, inside a module or inside a class. Consider this:

```ruby
class Person
  using(OnlySpace)

  def initialize (name)
    @name = name
  end

  def valid?
    !@name.only_space?
  end

  def display (io=$stdout)
    io.puts(@name)
  end
end
```

The using method expects a single argument, a module that contains refinements. The refinements in the module are activated, but only for the current lexical scope. This is an important feature and the reason why refinements are safer than monkey patching. Instead of patching a class and making those changes globally visible, refinements automatically deactivate outside of the lexical scope in which they were activated. Clearly, the only_space? method is available on strings *inside* the Person class. But what about the display method and the string it passes to puts? Here's the cool part: Once control leaves display and enters puts, the refinements defined in OnlySpace are deactivated. The puts method can't call only_space? on the string because that method is no longer available.

It makes sense that puts can't use the refinements activated in the Person class. But you may be wondering why I made it a point to say "lexical scope" over and over again in the previous paragraph. Obviously, it's important. The lexical scoping rules are stricter than you might think. For example, if you defined a Customer class that inherits from Person, you would *not* be able to use only_space? from within Customer just because its parent class can. Refinements aren't scoped that way. In this example, if you invoked the valid? method on a Customer object it would indeed work correctly since that method is defined in Person. But any methods defined directly in the Customer class cannot call only_space? without the refinement being activated in Customer first. (For a refresher on the lexical scoping rules take a look at Item 11.)

Just like anything in software development, you should use the simplest technique that will get the job done. If you can get away with something like the StringExtra class, prefer that over refinements. If you can't resist the temptation to monkey patch one of the core classes, then at least protect those around you with one of these techniques.

Things to Remember

✦ While refinements might not be experimental anymore, they're still subject to change as the feature matures.

✦ A refinement must be activated in each lexical scope in which you want to use it.

Item 33: Invoke Modified Methods with Alias Chaining

Back when I programmed on Motorola 68k processors running Macintosh System 7, I would use a pretty neat hack to replace parts of the operating system with my own code. System 7 had a dispatch table in RAM where it would look up the RAM or ROM locations of system code. I remember working on an application that needed to monitor key press events, even when it wasn't the active application. You couldn't do this directly so a really common workaround back then was to patch the system dispatch table.

The technique was simple enough. You started by searching through the dispatch table and finding the entry for the system function that handled keyboard events. Then you stashed away the function's address somewhere in your running application. Finally, you installed a new entry with an address that points to your code. (System 7 didn't have protected memory so an application could write into any RAM location, including the system heap.) When a key was pressed, the operating system would look in the dispatch table, find your address, and then invoke your code instead of the system function. Since you had the location of the original system function you could resume normal key processing by invoking the function at the stored location.

As a matter of fact, this technique was so common that when you fetched the address of the system function from the dispatch table, sometimes it did not actually refer to the actual system function. Another application might have already patched the dispatch table and inserted its address in place of the original. Each application that modified the dispatch table formed a call chain where one function would invoke the next function until the original operating-system function was finally called and the chain ended. (Apple itself used this technique to patch bugs that were burned into the system ROM.)

If you think of method names as being addresses to some chunk of code you want to run, it becomes clear that this sort of thing is possible in Ruby too. That's because you can use alias_method to give an existing method a new name. You can then call the method by its old name *and* its new name. But if you then redefine that method and give it a new implementation, you'll still be able invoke the original implementation through its other name. So you can hijack a method like in my dispatch table example and eventually call the real version. This is referred to as *alias chaining*. Let's take a look at an example.

Suppose you want to enhance a method in one of the core classes so it outputs logging information each time it's called. You don't want to change its behavior in any way, you just want to wrap around it so you can log when it's called and when it's finished. Sounds like a good use of alias chaining to me.

Even though it's a form of monkey patching, what allows alias chaining to avoid the downsides discussed in Item 30 is that it can be undone and usually doesn't alter the behavior of the target class in a way that will affect other code. Let's take a look at a module that can be used to add logging capabilities to any method, in any class:

```ruby
module LogMethod
  def log_method (method)
    # Choose a new, unique name for the method.
    orig = "#{method}_without_logging".to_sym

    # Make sure name is unique.
    if instance_methods.include?(orig)
      raise(NameError, "#{orig} isn't a unique name")
    end

    # Create a new name for the original method.
    alias_method(orig, method)

    # Replace original method.
    define_method(method) do |*args, &block|
      $stdout.puts("calling method '#{method}'")
      result = send(orig, *args, &block)
      $stdout.puts("'#{method}' returned #{result.inspect}")
      result
    end
  end
end
```

When a class is extended with the LogMethod module, it will receive a new class method named log_method. You can use log_method to wrap any existing method so that it outputs messages before and after it invokes the original method. Before we dig into the details let's see it in action:

```
irb> Array.extend(LogMethod)

irb> Array.log_method(:first)

irb> [1, 2, 3].first
calling method 'first'
'first' returned 1
---> 1

irb> %w(a b c).first_without_logging
---> "a"
```

Before redefining the target method, log_method uses alias_method to create a new name for it. The first argument to alias_method is the new name you want to create and the second argument is the existing name. After alias_method is called the method will be available by both names. Then log_method redefines the method using define_method, giving it a new implementation that performs the logging and uses the aliased name to invoke the original method. It's like my Macintosh hacking days all over again. Unfortunately, the LogMethod module isn't as safe as patching the good old dispatch table in System 7.

One thing you'll want to ensure is that the new name you create with alias_method is unique. If a method already exists with that name you'll clobber it without so much as a warning. That's why log_method raises an exception if the aliased name already exists. This version is also a bit simplistic and can't be used with operators. If you passed ":*" as the method name to log_method, it would try to create an alias named ":*_without_logging". Obviously that's not going to work. If you're looking for something more elaborate and robust you might consider continuously generating method names with a random component until you find one that isn't already defined. The technique you choose for generating the aliased name will depend on your particular needs.

A final feature to consider is adding a method that can put things back to the way they were originally. This usually involves a call to alias_method to restore the original implementation and a couple of calls to remove_method to delete the patched version and aliased name. Consider unlog_method:

```
module LogMethod
  def unlog_method (method)
    orig = "#{method}_without_logging".to_sym
```

```
  # Make sure log_method was called first.
  if !instance_methods.include?(orig)
    raise(NameError, "was #{orig} already removed?")
  end

  # Remove the logging version.
  remove_method(method)

  # Put the method back to its original name.
  alias_method(method, orig)

  # Remove the name created by log_method.
  remove_method(orig)
  end
end
```

Alias chaining is an interesting way to intercept method calls. As long as each link in the chain uses a unique name with alias_method, the original method can eventually be called through the chain.

Things to Remember

✦ When setting up an alias chain, make sure the aliased named is unique.

✦ Consider providing a method that can undo the alias chaining.

Item 34: Consider Supporting Differences in Proc Arity

Instances of the Proc class are ubiquitous in Ruby. Off the top of my head I can think of at least seven different ways to create Proc objects. And that's saying a lot since I have the attention span of a block argument. (That's right folks...enjoy the comedy while you can.) The most idiomatic way to create a Proc object is by passing a block to a method. While the block itself is just Ruby syntax, it eventually gets wrapped up in a Proc and passed to the method. We can see this directly if we write a method that accepts a block and then passes that block through as its return value:

```
irb> def pass (&block) block; end

irb> greeter = pass {|name| "Hello #{name}"}
---> #<Proc>

irb> greeter.call("World")
---> "Hello World"
```

The pass method takes a block and binds it to the variable block, then simply returns it. What is actually bound to the block variable is an instance of the Proc class. Like all good objects, you can send it messages, call being one of them. Creating Proc objects this way is the most common way, but not the only one. There are the proc and lambda methods, the Proc::new method, lambda syntax literals, and several other ways I could continue to enumerate (and bore us both to death). The reason I even bring this up is because all these various ways of creating a Proc object can be divided into two categories I'll call *weak* and *strong*. The major differences between weak and strong Proc objects are how they deal with invalid arguments. (They also differ in how they're affected by control-flow expressions. I won't go into that here, but any introductory book on Ruby should cover it.)

Weak Proc objects play fast and loose with their arguments. Calling a weak Proc object with the wrong number of arguments doesn't raise an exception or produce a warning. If you give too few arguments the missing ones will be set to nil. If you give too many arguments the extras are ignored. This is much different than how strong Proc objects behave. Calling a strong Proc object obeys all the rules of a normal method call. If the given number of arguments isn't exactly correct, an ArgumentError exception will be raised. Blocks turn into weak Proc objects and lambdas into strong. It's pretty easy to see this in action:

```
irb> def test
       # Yield one argument.
       yield("a")
     end

irb> test {|x, y, z| [x, y, z]} # Expect 3.
---> ["a", nil, nil]

irb> test {"b"} # Expect 0.
---> "b"

irb> func = ->(x) {"Hello #{x}"} # Expect 1.
---> #<Proc>

irb> func.call("a", "b") # Send 2.
ArgumentError: wrong number of arguments (2 for 1)
```

You can distinguish between weak and strong Proc objects using the lambda? method. It returns false for weak Proc objects and true for strong. This can be helpful in methods that accept blocks because they may receive weak *or* strong blocks, depending on how they're called. For example:

```
irb> def test (&block)
       block.lambda?
     end
```

```
irb> test {|x| x}
---> false
```

```
irb> test(& ->(x){x})
---> true
```

Knowing whether a Proc is weak or strong isn't in itself very useful. That is to say, it's not likely that you'll want to treat them differently based solely on their type. But knowing that strong Proc objects raise exceptions if they are called with the wrong number of arguments is good motivation for knowing how many arguments they expect. Let me illustrate this with an example. Suppose you've written a class for streaming data from an I/O object to a Proc. The class feeds the Proc data in chunks until the input has been exhausted. You also keep track of how many seconds it takes to read each chunk, just in case the Proc wants to calculate throughput. Consider this:

```
class Stream
  def initialize (io=$stdin, chunk=64*1024)
    @io, @chunk = io, chunk
  end

  def stream (&block)
    loop do
      start = Time.now
      data = @io.read(@chunk)
      return if data.nil?

      time = (Time.now - start).to_f
      block.call(data, time)
    end
  end
end
```

The stream method will always give the Proc object two arguments: the data that was read and the timing information. If the Proc doesn't want it—and it's a weak Proc—it just ignores the argument.

Consider this naive (and inefficient) method for calculating the size of a file:

```
def file_size (file)
  File.open(file) do |f|
    bytes = 0

    s = Stream.new(f)
    s.stream {|data| bytes += data.size}

    bytes
  end
end
```

By always yielding two arguments to the Proc object you're limiting yourself to weak Proc objects or alternatively, strong Proc objects that declare an argument that goes unused. But you can't always control how many arguments a Proc expects. What if you wanted to pass a method to stream instead of a block and that method only accepted a single argument? For example, here's a method that uses the Stream class to generate a SHA256 cryptographic hash:

```
require('digest')

def digest (file)
  File.open(file) do |f|
    sha = Digest::SHA256.new
    s = Stream.new(f)
    s.stream(&sha.method(:update))
    sha.hexdigest
  end
end
```

The Digest::SHA256 class has a method called update that allows you to supply data in chunks instead of having to read an entire file into memory. It expects one argument: a string containing the next chunk to add to the hash. We can use the "&" operator within a method invocation to turn the update method into a strong Proc object. But with the Stream class the way it is now, passing the update method to stream will raise an exception because it's passing two arguments to the Proc instead of one.

Wouldn't it be nice if we knew how many arguments the Proc object expected? That's where the Proc#arity method comes in. It returns a Fixnum that contains the number of arguments the

Proc object expects to be given. Well, almost.... If only it were that simple. Recall that methods can have default arguments, making them optional. So what should arity return in that case? A method might also have a variadic argument by using "*" to collect all remaining arguments into a single array, basically making the method's arity infinite. In these cases, the arity method will return a negative Fixnum that tells you indirectly how many arguments are required.

I say indirect because the negative Fixnum is actually the ones' complement of the number of required arguments. If a method had one mandatory argument and one optional argument then arity would return -2. You can use the unary complement operator ("~") to turn that result into the number of required arguments:

```
irb> func = ->(x, y=1) {x+y}

irb> func.arity
---> -2

irb> ~ func.arity
---> 1
```

Now we can rewrite the stream method so that it only gives the timing information to Proc objects that are expecting two arguments:

```
def stream (&block)
  loop do
    start = Time.now
    data = @io.read(@chunk)
    return if data.nil?

    arg_count = block.arity
    arg_list = [data]

    if arg_count == 2 || ~arg_count == 2
      arg_list << (Time.now - start).to_f
    end

    block.call(*arg_list)
  end
end
```

And with that change the digest method can now pass the Digest::SHA256#update method as a Proc object to the stream method. Being able to use strong Proc objects this way is a neat trick and something you should consider when writing methods that take blocks.

Things to Remember

✦ Unlike weak Proc objects, their strong counterparts will raise an ArgumentError exception if called with the wrong number of arguments.

✦ You can use the Proc#arity method to find out how many arguments a Proc object expects. A positive number means it expects that exact number of arguments. A negative number, on the other hand, means there are optional arguments and it is the ones' complement of the number of required arguments.

Item 35: Think Carefully Before Using Module Prepending

Back in Item 6 we looked into Ruby's internals to see how including modules into a class altered the inheritance hierarchy. Recall that when you use the include method from within a class, Ruby creates a singleton class to hold the module's methods and inserts it as an invisible superclass. When multiple modules are included into a class they are found by the method-dispatching algorithm in reverse order. An example makes this easier to visualize:

```ruby
module A
  def who_am_i?
    "A#who_am_i?"
  end
end

module B
  def who_am_i?
    "B#who_am_i?"
  end
end

class C
  include(A)
  include(B)

  def who_am_i?
    "C#who_am_i?"
  end
end
```

The two modules (A and B) are included into the C class. All three define a method named who_am_i? to help us see how the different implementations override one another based on the include order. We can also use the ancestors class method to get an idea of how the class hierarchy is constructed and which method would be invoked if we called super from within each of the who_am_i? methods. Consider this:

```
irb> C.ancestors
---> [C, B, A, Object, Kernel, BasicObject]

irb> C.new.who_am_i?
---> "C#who_am_i?"
```

As you'd expect, methods defined in C come before those included from the modules. And since the include method inserts modules between the C class and its superclass, the B module comes before A in the search order. Based on the output from the ancestors method we can see that if the C#who_am_i? method used super it would invoke the B#who_am_i? method. The ordering is really important because it allows you to emulate multiple inheritance while retaining the ability to override specific methods in the class that is doing the including, just like you can with a traditional parent class. In other words, methods defined in the class take priority over any methods higher up in the hierarchy (pretty standard object-oriented behavior). But it's not the only way a module can appear in the class hierarchy.

Starting in Ruby 2.0 you can use the prepend method as another way to insert a module into the inheritance hierarchy. It looks and feels just like the include method. It even has its own module hook called prepended. But prepend works much differently than include. While include inserts a list of modules between the receiver and its superclass, prepend inserts them *before* the receiver. That's right, *before*. This makes for some very surprising changes to method dispatching. Let's change the C class to use prepend instead of include and see what happens:

```
class C
  prepend(A)
  prepend(B)

  def who_am_i?
    "C#who_am_i?"
  end
end
irb> C.ancestors
---> [B, A, C, Object, Kernel, BasicObject]

irb> C.new.who_am_i?
---> "B#who_am_i?"
```

After prepending the A and B modules into the C class you can see that they show up before C in the list of ancestors. Calling the who_am_i? method on an instance of C will therefore trigger the implementation in the B module first, before the definition in C is even seen. The biggest side effect of prepending is that you can no longer override a module's method by simply defining a version in the class. The definition in the class is overridden by the module and will only be invoked if the module's method calls super. This goes against the grain of most object-oriented languages because method dispatch will start *below* the object's class in the hierarchy and only make its way upward to the class if the method isn't found or super is used.

You might be wondering if prepending a module is useful or not. For the most part it gives us a second way of doing things we could already do without it. Take method alias chaining from Item 33, for example. We used alias_method to create a new name for an existing method so we could redefine it with a new implementation but retain the ability to invoke the original implementation. This is analogous to prepending a module in order to redefine a method and then using super to access the original. But I prefer using alias_method because it's easy to put things back the way they were by using it a second time to restore the original implementation. There's no way to do the same thing with prepend. Removing a module once it's been prepended isn't possible.

Overall, using prepend to add a module to a class leaves the inheritance hierarchy in a nonintuitive state. If you're going to use it, think very carefully about how it affects method dispatching before proceeding.

Things to Remember

+ Using the prepend method inserts a module *before* the receiver in the class hierarchy, which is much different than include, which inserts a module between the receiver and its superclass.

+ Similar to the included and extended module hooks, prepending a module triggers the prepended hook.

Testing

Testing is an important part of software development, especially with dynamic languages like Ruby. Ensuring that your code works as specified is one of the most critical parts of building a successful product. Projects that skip testing often collapse under the uncertainty that small changes might introduce unwanted and unanticipated side effects.

Ruby comes with a testing framework in its standard library, and there are many testing libraries available as RubyGems. This chapter will show you how to use these tools to write effective tests. While testing doesn't offer proof that your code is free of bugs, it does increase your confidence that you've found many of them before your customers do.

Item 36: Familiarize Yourself with MiniTest Unit Testing

While there are all sorts of fancy testing frameworks available for Ruby, there's something refreshing about the easy-to-use alternative known as MiniTest. It has been distributed with Ruby since version 1.9 and continues to get better with each successive version. There's nothing to install—you just have to require a file and write a test case. I think that's a big win for MiniTest *and* Ruby.

MiniTest replaced an existing standard testing framework known as TestUnit. One of the really nice things about MiniTest is that it includes a compatibility shim that emulates the TestUnit interface. This means that if you find yourself updating older code to work with newer versions of Ruby, you can leave the existing TestUnit tests alone and they'll work just fine.

In addition to being one of Ruby's standard library packages, MiniTest is also an independent RubyGem. If you need a newer version of MiniTest and can't upgrade Ruby itself, you can always add an external dependency to your project (see Item 42). But the majority of the time you won't need to do this. The unit-testing component of MiniTest is very stable and hasn't changed much from version to version. That said, some of MiniTest's advanced features have been greatly improved over the years, and you may need to upgrade to take advantage of them. (Mocking is one such feature, which we'll look at in Item 38.)

Getting started with MiniTest is easy. Traditionally, each test case is written into its own file and covers a single "unit" of code. In Ruby, that's often a single class. Let's write a test case that validates the features of a class we've already seen.

Back in Item 13 we played with the `Version` class for parsing and comparing version numbers. Given a string containing a version number, the `Version::new` method returns a new object that can be used to access the individual components of a version number: major, minor, and patch level. We can also compare two version objects using the standard comparison operators. Assuming that the `Version` class is defined in a file named "version.rb", it's common practice to store its test case in a file named "version_test.rb" within a "test" or "tests" directory. It's also fairly common to call the file "test_version.rb". Choose the naming convention you like best and the one that fits into any application frameworks you might be using. (For example, Ruby on Rails prefers the "_test" suffix.)

The first step when using MiniTest is to require the appropriate library file. There are a handful of files you can choose from depending on which specific features you plan on using. But most of the time it's easiest to load the entire library, which also brings in some glue code to automatically execute any tests you define in the test case file:

```
require('minitest/autorun')
```

The "autorun" file begins by loading the three major components of the MiniTest library: unit testing, spec testing, and mocking. It then registers itself with Ruby so that after all tests have been defined they will be executed. This means you don't have to do anything special to run your tests, you just have to execute the file they're defined in.

After the MiniTest library is loaded the next step is to define a class to represent the test case. The name of the class isn't important (it's usually named after the file), but it does need to use `MiniTest::Unit::TestCase` as its superclass. Since we're testing the `Version` class and the tests are in the "version_test.rb" file, we'll call the class `VersionTest`:

```
class VersionTest < MiniTest::Unit::TestCase
  ...
end
```

Now comes the fun part—writing the actual testing logic. Individual tests are written as instance methods whose names must begin with the "test_" prefix. How you divide the test case up into individual test methods is entirely up to you. Typically, you'll want each test method to be as small as possible. Just like any method, this makes it easier to troubleshoot and maintain. Smaller methods can also shed light on test-ordering dependencies—tests that only work when called in a specific order—since MiniTest randomizes the methods before executing each test case. Let's start with a simple test to see if the Version class can properly parse the major version number out of a string:

```ruby
def test_major_number
  v = Version.new("2.1.3")
  assert(v.major == 2, "major should be 2")
end
```

This method shows how to actually get something tested, through assertions. There are a lot of assertion methods to choose from, but the easiest is the assert method. It has one mandatory argument, a value that should be true. If the argument is true then the assertion passes and the code continues along its normal path. But if the value is not true then the assertion halts the current test method and reports a failure. In this case, the optional second argument can be used to give additional details about why the assertion failed.

While you could certainly stick with the simple assert method for all of your assertions, there's a good reason to explore the MiniTest::Assertions module documentation and use more specific assertions. The more appropriate the assertion is for your test, the better the error message will be when an assertion fails. The plain assert method relies on its second argument to provide a meaningful failure message. Other assertion methods can automatically report what was being tested, what was expected, and what actually happened. It also makes your test methods more succinct. Let's rewrite the previous test method with a different assertion and expand it to test other components of a version number:

```ruby
def test_can_parse_version_string
  v = Version.new("2.1.3")
  assert_equal(2, v.major, "major")
  assert_equal(1, v.minor, "minor")
  assert_equal(3, v.patch, "patch")
end
```

The assert_equal method takes two mandatory arguments, and like assert, an optional message that is displayed for failures. The first argument is the expected value and the second is the actual value. It might not seem like the order of the two arguments matters much, but it turns out to be quite useful for the assertion failure message. Let's look at a test method that intentionally fails so we can see the message produced by assert_equal:

```
def test_force_assertion_failure
  v = Version.new("3.8.11")
  assert_equal(4, v.major, "parsing major")
end
```

```
VersionTest#test_force_assertion_failure:
parsing major.
Expected: 4
  Actual: 3
```

Each assertion method generates its own failure message that incorporates the optional description given as its last argument. This makes it easy to understand why an assertion is failing. Before you go too far with MiniTest make sure you read the documentation and familiarize yourself with the available assertion methods. As I mentioned previously, they're documented in the MiniTest::Assertions module.

Sometimes you may notice a lot of duplication among your test methods, especially in the steps they take to prepare the objects to be tested. There are two main ways to deal with this. First, since MiniTest will only invoke methods whose names begin with "test_", you're free to write helper methods in your test case, which can then be called from the test methods. It's common practice to mark these methods as private to further indicate that they won't be called directly by MiniTest. The second way is more automated. If you define a method named setup, it will be invoked *before* each test method. Its partner, the teardown method, is called *after* each test method finishes. Typically, you'll use the setup method to create some test objects that get assigned to instance variables. Then each of the test methods can use them directly. Here's an example:

```
def setup
  @v1 = Version.new("2.1.1")
  @v2 = Version.new("2.3.0")
end
```

```
def test_version_compare
  refute_equal(@v1, @v2)
  assert_operator(@v1, :<, @v2)
end
```

You might have noticed that the test_version_compare method used a method called refute_equal. Nearly all of the assertion methods have matching refutations that negate their test. For example, the refute_equal method *fails* if its first two arguments are the same (when compared with the "==" operator), which is the opposite of assert_equal. Again, this is mostly useful for producing meaningful failure messages without having to manually write specific details into every test. Each of the refutation methods are documented along with the assertion methods in the MiniTest::Assertions module.

When you have more than a single test file you should find a way to run all of your tests from a single location. Because let's face it: Tests that don't get run aren't of much use. The most common way to group all of your tests into a single command is by using a tool that is part of every Ruby installation: Rake. Frameworks like Ruby on Rails already provide a configuration file for Rake that can execute all of your tests. But writing one of these files yourself is pretty easy:

```ruby
require('rake/testtask')
Rake::TestTask.new do |t|
  t.test_files = FileList['test/*_test.rb']
  t.warning = true # Turn on Ruby warnings.
end
```

Putting these lines into a file named "Rakefile" will give you everything you need to execute all of the test files. Rake will use the shell pattern given to the FileList class to find test files and execute them. You probably noticed that a "Rakefile" is really just Ruby code, which means you don't have to learn a new language to use Rake. With just these few lines in place you can run "rake test" from your favorite shell and watch all of your tests execute.

Things to Remember

+ Test methods must begin with the "test_" prefix.

+ Keep your test methods short to help with troubleshooting and maintenance.

+ Use the most appropriate assertions possible to get better failure messages.

+ Assertions and refutations are documented in the MiniTest:: Assertions module.

Item 37: Familiarize Yourself with MiniTest Spec Testing

Many testing methodologies have emerged over the past few decades. The Ruby community is mostly divided between two major testing paradigms: unit testing (often associated with test-driven development) and spec testing (more formally referred to as behavioral specification and associated with behavior-driven development). Spec tests can be divided into two styles of behavioral specification: those written in a formal language that is shared by programmers and nonprogrammers alike and those written in the syntax of the hosting programming language. The previous item dealt with unit testing using the MiniTest framework, but this item focuses on using the spec interface for writing behavioral specifications in Ruby. If you haven't read Item 36 you should do so before continuing. This item builds off ideas and terminology introduced during our study of unit testing.

Spec testing in MiniTest is done through a thin wrapper around its unit-testing interface and mostly provides an alternative style for writing tests. So we won't go into any specific details about behavior-driven development, but instead will focus on this alternate interface for writing unit tests.

As with the previous item, we'll use the Version class that was developed in Item 13 as the subject for our tests. Let's jump right in and explore the previously written unit test for the Version class, this time implemented as spec tests:

```
require('minitest/autorun')
describe(Version) do
  describe("when parsing") do
    before do
      @version = Version.new("10.8.9")
    end

    it("creates three integers") do
      @version.major.must_equal(10)
      @version.minor.must_equal(8)
      @version.patch.must_equal(9)
    end
  end

  describe("when comparing") do
    before do
      @v1 = Version.new("2.1.1")
      @v2 = Version.new("2.3.0")
    end

    it("orders correctly") do
      @v1.wont_equal(@v2)
      @v1.must_be(:<, @v2)
    end
  end
end
```

Notice that the very first line uses require to load the entire MiniTest library. It's the same require from the previous item, which means that executing this file with the Ruby interpreter will cause MiniTest to execute all of the tests defined within it. This is a common way to load the MiniTest library regardless of which style of testing you happen to be performing.

I pointed out the require line specifically because I'm willing to bet your eyes jumped right to the describe method and that you probably noticed there's no class definition. Also missing are the top-level assertion methods we used in the unit-testing item. They've been replaced by method calls that begin with "must_", which is indeed pretty strange. I'll tackle these one at a time.

Each invocation of the describe method automatically defines a new class that inherits from MiniTest::Spec. While you can certainly define your own class directly like we did when working with the unit-testing interface, it's much more common to use the describe method to define the class indirectly. The argument given to the describe method can be any object. It's converted into a string and used as an internal label for the new, anonymous class. This label is included with test-failure messages similar to how the unit-testing interface uses the class name. As you can see from the example, the describe method is given a block that is used to nest additional describe methods for more context in failure messages. The outer describe method is usually given the class name that is being tested, and the nested describe methods are given strings that provide human-readable messages about the context in which the test is taking place. You don't have to nest describe methods...one is enough. You're also free to add as much context through them as you need.

The before method can be used inside a describe block and acts just like the setup method from MiniTest unit testing. There's also an after method that corresponds to the unit testing teardown method. Both before and after take blocks that are evaluated before and after each test, respectively. In the example spec test, the before method is used to create Version objects and store them in instance variables so they can be used by each of the tests in the same describe block. And that brings us to the actual testing.

A test is defined using the it method. Like describe, the it method takes a description that is used in failure messages and a block where the actual testing takes place. In spec testing, assertions have been replaced with some monkey patching that allows you to call methods like must_equal on any object. The assertion methods we used in the unit-testing item are still available in spec tests, but in spec tests it's more common to use what are called "expectations." These are the familiar assertion methods injected into the Object class with new names, which are documented in the MiniTest::Expectations module. The refutations from the unit-testing interface are also available in spec testing; those methods begin with "wont_". In the example above, you can see wont_equal, which is the same as the refutation refute_equal.

There's not much more to it than that. Under the hood, spec testing and unit testing with MiniTest are very similar. The one you choose is mostly a matter of taste. If you like the style of testing offered by the MiniTest spec-testing interface, you might want to take a look at the RSpec or the Cucumber RubyGems, which take behavior-driven development much further than MiniTest.

Things to Remember

✦ Use the describe method to create a testing class and the it method to define your tests.

✦ While assertion methods are still available, spec tests generally use expectation methods that are injected into the Object class.

✦ Expectations are documented in the MiniTest::Expectations module.

Item 38: Simulate Determinism with Mock Objects

Suppose you've written a monitoring program that can report the status of servers in production. It does this by sending an HTTP request to each server with data the server should echo back. If the HTTP request is successful and the response contains the correct echo data, then the server is considered to be alive and healthy. Let's take a look at the class responsible for making and verifying the HTTP request:

```ruby
require('uri')

class Monitor
  def initialize (server)
    @server = server
  end

  def alive?
    echo = Time.now.to_f.to_s
    response = get(echo)
    response.success? && response.body == echo
  end

  private
  def get (echo)
    url = URI::HTTP.build(host: @server,
                          path: "/echo/#{echo}")
```

```
    HTTP.get(url.to_s)
  end
end
```

There are two interesting parts to this class. The `Monitor#get` method constructs a URL and then initiates an HTTP request. All the heavy lifting is in the HTTP class (which isn't shown here). The `HTTP::get` method takes a URL and returns an object that contains all the information we need to know to determine the status of the server. The `Monitor#alive?` method uses this response object to test if the request was successful and whether the correct echo data was included in the response body. So far, so good.

Now you'd like to test this `Monitor` class. You could certainly write a unit test with some assertions to ensure the `Monitor#alive?` method works correctly, but what if one of the production servers is offline while the tests are running? Along the same lines, what if you wanted to pretend that one of the servers is offline to make sure that `Monitor#alive?` returns `false`?

This sort of thing comes up all the time in testing. If at all possible, it's best to isolate your tests from the nondeterminism of the outside world. This allows you to simulate successful and unsuccessfully conditions to ensure your code can correctly handle both. This extends beyond network services. It's important to test situations like disks filling up and February having an extra day due to a leap year. The way we handle this in our tests is through mocking, and as we'll see, a pinch of metaprogramming.

With test mocking you can build objects that respond in any way you need. Mock objects (also called *test doubles*) stand in for code that is nondeterministic but for which you need specific results. The HTTP class is a good candidate for mocking. We don't want the unit tests to make connections to the production servers every time they run, and we certainly don't want the tests to depend on the state of the servers either. Instead, we'd like to create HTTP response objects that can simulate healthy and unhealthy servers.

One of the downsides to mocking is that we're no longer testing just the interface of a class...we're exploiting specific details about its implementation. This is known as white-box testing (as opposed to black-box testing), and the unit tests will be coupled to a specific implementation of the class. If we mock the response object from the `HTTP::get` method and then later the `Monitor` class starts using a different HTTP library, the tests might silently start using the network again instead of a simulated network.

To combat this problem, mocking libraries support something called *expectations*. Not only can we simulate specific conditions with mock objects, but we can also require that certain methods be called during the lifetime of the mock object. If the expected methods are not invoked during the test, it will be considered a failure. Expectations also allow us to ensure that methods on a mock object are called with specific arguments and return specific results.

The MiniTest library we've been exploring throughout this chapter comes with a simple and easy-to-use class for mocking. Let's use it to simulate successful and unsuccessfully HTTP requests to the production servers. We don't need to do anything special to use the MiniTest mocking class. Assuming we already have a test class similar to the one in Item 36, let's take a look at a test method that uses mocking:

```ruby
def test_successful_monitor
  monitor = Monitor.new("example.com")
  response = MiniTest::Mock.new

  monitor.define_singleton_method(:get) do |echo|
    response.expect(:success?, true)
    response.expect(:body, echo)
    response
  end

  assert(monitor.alive?, "should be alive")
  response.verify
end
```

The MiniTest::Mock::new method returns a blank object that is ready and eager to pretend to be any other object. Since the Monitor#get method deals with all of the HTTP work it's the ideal method to replace using define_singleton_method. Mock objects respond to the expect method, which takes at least two arguments. The first is a symbol, which is the name of the method that is expected to be called. The second is the return value for that method. The monkey-patched get method creates two expectations on the mocked object: its success? method will return true and its body method will return the echo data. Exactly what we need to simulate a successful connection and healthy server. After setting up some expectations, the get method returns the mocked response object back to its caller, just like the real Monitor#get method does.

When Monitor#alive? is invoked it will call the get method and then use the mocked response object to determine if it should return true or false. Since the get singleton method always returns a successful response the tests should always pass (as long as alive? is doing the right thing).

Did you notice the call to response.verify at the end of the test method? This is an important step in using MiniTest mock objects.

When you call MiniTest::Mock#verify the mock object confirms that all expected methods were called. If any of the expected methods were not called, the verify method will raise an exception that will cause the tests to fail.

The next test we need to write should simulate a failed HTTP request. This is where the beauty of mocking starts to show. We can create a response that looks like a network failure regardless of the current network status. This test method is even simpler than the successful case:

```ruby
def test_failed_monitor
  monitor = Monitor.new("example.com")
  response = MiniTest::Mock.new

  monitor.define_singleton_method(:get) do |echo|
    response.expect(:success?, false)
    response
  end

  refute(monitor.alive?, "shouldn't be alive")
  response.verify
end
```

This test definitely exploits our knowledge of the alive? method's internal implementation. Unlike with the successful mock object, in the failure case we don't create an expectation for the body method. If the implementation of the alive? method changed and it started calling the body method on the response object even when success? returned false, this test would raise a NoMethodError explaining that an unmocked method was called (yet another benefit of explicit expectations on mock objects).

With a little bit of metaprogramming you can do quite a bit with the MiniTest::Mock class. Everything shown in this item will work with all of the MiniTest versions shipped since Ruby 1.9.3. But MiniTest mocking has undergone some improvements over the years and you may want to consider using the RubyGem version over the one packaged with Ruby. That said, it's a very simple mocking library that isn't very sophisticated compared to other mocking libraries. One of my favorite libraries is Mocha, which is available as a RubyGem. Mocha allows you to do everything MiniTest::Mock can do and a whole lot more. MiniTest is nice because it's bundled with Ruby, but if you find yourself outgrowing it there are plenty of other options available as RubyGems.

I'll end with a final word of warning. Earlier I mentioned that one of the downsides to mocking is the fact that we need to exploit the internal workings of a class. In the case of the presented example, the test code replaced the internal get method with one that prepared and returned a mock object instead of a real result. This means that the actual get method from the Monitor class might contain bugs that go untested. When using mocking it's best to mock methods provided by code from outside of your project (gems, the Ruby core library, etc.). For this example, that might be the HTTP::get method or possibly even the Ruby networking API. This sort of mocking is much easier with gems like Mocha that undo any changes made by mocking when a test completes. Just remember that mocking or replacing a method might lead to untested code that could fail in production.

Things to Remember

✦ Use mocking to isolate tests from the nondeterminism of the outside world.

✦ Mocking or replacing a method might lead to untested code that could fail in production.

✦ Be sure to call MiniTest::Mock#verify before the end of the test method.

Item 39: Strive for Effectively Tested Code

Ruby has a lot going for it. Each of us came to the language for different reasons, but I'm willing to bet there's a lot of overlap between them. For me, the best way I can describe my first experience with Ruby is that it was fun. The syntax was really easy to learn and behind it was a consistent language that, compared to most other languages, didn't appear to have any dark corners, places where even experts feared to tread. You know, those strange parts of other languages where some odd construct is allowed but produces undefined behavior, something you probably have to end up learning the hard way.

I would venture to say that most Ruby programmers consider working with the language to be a joy. I've been to a lot of Ruby get-togethers and the meetings are always electric with enthusiasm from everyone involved. But that doesn't mean that Ruby doesn't have a darker side. The same features that make Ruby so great also produce sharp edges that are not always easy to recognize. Being an interpreted language, everything in Ruby happens at run time. Even simple mistakes like typos can't be found without actually executing your code. Consider this:

```
w = Widget.new
w.seed(:name)
```

If I were seeing this code for the first time I would wonder if the Widget class actually responds to the seed message. But let's say you were able to read the definition of the Widget class and there was no seed method to be found. Does that mean that you can't send the seed message to the Widget object? What if that method was monkey patched into the Widget class or the Kernel module? What if that method only existed after loading a specific library? What I'm getting at is that it's *really* hard to tell if Widget#seed is a real method or just a typo. (Could the author have meant to type send instead of seed?) The only way to know for sure is to run the code and see what happens. Let's look at something similar:

```
def update (location)
  @status = location.description
end
```

We could ask all the same questions from earlier about this location object and the description method, but here are few new ones. What is a location? What if the location object isn't of the expected class, or worse, what if it's nil? Is there a way for us to be warned that location might not be what we think it is? The only way to know for sure is to run the code. And so, as Ruby programmers, that's what we do—we run the code. We just do it in a controlled way, by writing tests that execute our code and hopefully verify that it works correctly. We write tests to make sure we don't have any syntax errors in our code, to make sure we haven't accidentally introduced typos, and just as important, to make sure the business logic we're weaving into the code conforms to its specification. But there's a lot more we should be doing.

Throughout this chapter we've mostly been performing functional testing, that is, confirming that the logic in the code behaves the way we expect it to. The beautiful part about writing tests is that we can run them as often as we like. They give us a baseline to work from so that after changing code we can verify that the changes haven't altered the code in such a way that it no longer behaves as expected. But this only works if we write tests that don't contain any bugs. I've worked with too many projects where the tests all continue to pass even when I sabotaged the code in a way that violated its specification. My point is that it's easy to write functional tests that pass even when they shouldn't.

I consider this to be one of the major motivating forces behind methodologies like test-driven development (TDD). On the surface it makes sense that writing a test before the implementation leads to better code *and* better tests. But in my experience it's still really easy to write tests that miss the mark and pass when they shouldn't. And with something like TDD, when the tests start to pass, it's supposed to be a signal that you're done and can move on to the next feature. Clearly, writing tests that actually verify that your code works as expected isn't as easy as it might first appear. Let's take a closer look at some ways our tests can be inadequate and what we can do about it.

A common mistake made in all forms of testing is only performing *happy path* testing. This is especially common if you're writing tests for code you recently authored. Happy path testing is when you carefully establish all of the preconditions for the code you're testing and then provide only valid inputs to it. You're basically asking the question: "Does this code work in a perfect world?" But the world isn't perfect. Customers feed invalid data into our applications. We forget to validate an input field and a sloppy database schema allows a NULL value to slip in where it shouldn't. Testing the happy path is valuable but doesn't expose any of these bugs because we've tailored tests to only exercise the code in expected ways. One way to correct this is with *exception path* testing, that is, sending in various inputs and ensuring that all code branches are executed. But this can become very complicated, very fast. Fortunately, there are tools that can help us, namely, fuzz testing and property testing.

These two forms of testing are related but have different goals. The basic idea is that we want to feed many different types of data into our code and ensure that it holds up. Traditionally, fuzz testing was focused on security. Sending lots of random data into a program or a specific method is a great way to find out if it crashes or exposes a security hole. With fuzzing, our focus moves away from the idea of passing and failing and instead we look to see if we can cause some code to crash or raise an unexpected exception. The process usually involves a generator that produces random values and a piece of code we want to test. For example, suppose we want to know if the URI::HTTP::build method would crash if given completely random and invalid host names. To answer that question we can turn to Fuzz-Bert, one of the fuzzing libraries available for Ruby as a RubyGem:

```ruby
require('fuzzbert')
require('uri')

fuzz('URI::HTTP::build') do
  data("random server names") do
    FuzzBert::Generators.random
  end

  deploy do |data|
    URI::HTTP.build(host: data, path: '/')
  end
end
```

This fuzz test is made up of two parts: the generator and the test. The data block is used to configure the random data we want to use as host names. There are several types of generators available in FuzzBert. The random generator produces completely random values. And you're not limited to using a single data block—you can define as many as you want. This allows you to feed various types of random data into the code you're testing. The actual testing is done in the deploy block. This block is invoked over and over again and is yielded values from the generator. Notice that we don't test the return value from the URI::HTTP::build method; we're only concerned with it raising an exception or crashing the test program. FuzzBert goes to great lengths to run the fuzz testing in a separate process to detect if the fuzzing caused a crash.

Fuzz testing is definitely interesting, but it's not practical for everyday use. Part of this is because tools like FuzzBert run your fuzz tests continuously until you manually terminate them. For fuzz tests to be effective you should leave them running for several days. There are configuration options available to limit how long FuzzBert executes the tests, but the longer you let it run the more confident you can be that your code doesn't contain any crashing bugs.

Another way to exercise the happy *and* exception paths of your code is through property-based testing. Like fuzz testing, property testing involves sending random inputs into your code, but with the added test that the code should behave in a specified way. It is also much more practical than fuzz testing because the number of tests are finite and can be run along with your automated unit tests. To explore property testing let's turn our attention back to Item 13 where we wrote a Version class for parsing a version number out of a string. Previously, we focused on comparing different version numbers, but for now we'll only concern ourselves with parsing the version string. Here's a simplified Version class with an added method, to_s:

```ruby
class Version
  def initialize (version)
    @major, @minor, @patch =
      version.split('.').map(&:to_i)
  end

  def to_s
    [@major, @minor, @patch].join('.')
  end
end
```

When performing property-based testing you define properties that your code should satisfy and then a tool generates a large number of tests cases in an attempt to falsify the property. One easy way to come up with properties is to think of inverses. For the Version class, the initialize method turns a version string into three integers. The inverse of that is the to_s method, which takes those same three integers and turns them back into a version string. So one property of the Version class is that the string returned from the to_s method should have the same content as the string given to initialize. If they're not the same then there's a bug in either initialize or to_s. Let's use the MrProper RubyGem to define and test this property:

```
require('mrproper')

properties("Version") do
  data([Integer, Integer, Integer])

  property("new(str).to_s == str") do |data|
    str = data.join('.')
    assert_equal(str, Version.new(str).to_s)
  end
end
```

The data method is a lot like the data block we used with FuzzBert. It tells MrProper the type of random data we want to generate for the test cases. Since the property we're testing requires three integers, we can give the data method an array with three elements, all of which are the Integer class. MrProper will then generate random arrays of three integers and feed them into each of the property blocks. Since the properties are turned into MiniTest unit tests you can use all of the assertion methods you've come to know and love. For the Version class, the property block turns the three integers into a version string like "2.3.4." It then confirms that the to_s method can produce the same string. Property testing can help expose any assumptions that were written into your code. For example, if you assumed that a major version number would never be bigger than two digits then the MrProper example would fail by raising a MrProper::FalsableProperty exception.

Even after you've made an effort to test the happy and exception paths of your code, how do you know if you've succeeded? That's where test coverage tools like the SimpleCov RubyGem come in. Code-coverage tools generate reports that tell you which lines of your code were actually executed while the tests were running. SimpleCov produces detailed HTML reports that include all of the source code from your project with highlighting that shows executed lines in green and lines that were not executed in red. Test-code coverage analysis can be useful for guiding you while writing tests. Specifically, making sure you've exercised all branches of a particularly complex method. But it can also give you a false sense of security since *executed* code isn't necessarily *correct* code. You still need to make sure you're writing effective tests for branches you want to execute.

Using the SimpleCov tool is so simple that I won't go into it here. The website contains all the information you'll need for using it with any Ruby project, including Ruby on Rails applications. As long as you keep its downsides in mind and don't get lured into a false sense of security then coverage tools can be very helpful when writing tests.

Regardless of the tools you choose to use for testing, there are a few general rules you should follow. The most important is to write tests as soon as possible. Waiting until you're nearing the completion of a project is too late. It makes testing a separate project in and of itself and in the meantime you've likely forgotten some important properties you wanted to test. It's much easier to test a feature while you're writing it.

When you do write tests, make sure they fail. I like to comment out a critical section of code and check to see if the tests for it start failing. If they don't you've got a major problem with your tests. This goes hand in hand with bug finding. Before you start to search for the root cause of a bug, write a test that fails because of it. Reproducing the bug is the first step to fixing it, and having a test specifically for that bug means it should never return after it has been fixed.

Finally, automate your tests as much as possible. The best tests are useless if you don't run them. Some people like to configure their source code control system to reject a commit if the tests don't pass. You can also use a continuous integration tool to run your tests automatically when new commits are pushed up to a central repository. It can be fun to tease the developer who pushed changes that broke the tests.

You can also turn to tools like ZenTest, which watch your source code and automatically run the project's tests when a source file changes. Whichever method you choose, make sure you're actually running your tests and running them often. They're your last defense against preventable bugs showing up in production.

Things to Remember

+ Use fuzzing and property-based testing tools to help exercise both the happy *and* exception paths of your code.

+ Test-code coverage can give you a false sense of security since *executed* code isn't necessarily *correct* code.

+ It's much easier to test a feature while you're writing it.

+ Before you start to search for the root cause of a bug, write a test that fails because of it.

+ Automate your tests as much as possible.

7

Tools and Libraries

An installation of Ruby gives you more than just an interpreter to execute your source files with. It also includes an interactive tool for experimenting with Ruby (IRB), a utility for reading documentation (RI), and one for generating documentation (RDoc). Mastering these tools is an important step for Ruby programmers. But there's another equally important tool that ships with Ruby—the gem utility.

There's an amazingly large number of libraries and applications packaged as RubyGems just waiting to be installed with gem. In fact, it's quite common for Ruby applications to depend on many third-party gems. Managing all of those dependencies can be troublesome if you're not using a tool to help you.

In this chapter, I'll show you how to get the most from Ruby's standard tools such as IRB and RI as well as how to use the Bundler tool to manage your gem dependencies.

Item 40: Know How to Work with Ruby Documentation

Throughout our time together I've been telling you to consult the documentation for the so-and-so class or the whatsit module, but how do you do that? Where does this documentation come from? Can you document your own code in a similar way? Do I normally ask this many questions in a row?

The core and standard Ruby libraries come with excellent documentation and examples. Packaged along with Ruby are two tools for working with this documentation—let's tackle them one at a time. The first tool, RI, is a terminal-based tool for viewing "Ruby Information." With this tool you can view documentation for classes, modules, methods, and even the documentation for entire gems. Suppose you wanted to know more about the `Array` class. To view its documentation you just need to open a terminal window and ask RI:

```
ri Array
```

This command will bring up everything you ever wanted to know about the `Array` class, including any modules it includes and a list of its class and instance methods. You can even see if any installed gems have monkey patched the `Array` class, adding documented methods in the process. Here are some examples of the various types of queries you can ask the `ri` utility:

- `File::open` – The open class method of the `File` class.

- `Date::new` – The `new` class method of the `Date` class. This is a special case since the documentation for the `new` class method actually comes from the `initialize` instance method. (I'll talk more about this shortly.)

- `Time#hour` – The hour instance method of the `Time` class.

- `clear` – Any class or module that has a `clear` method will be listed with accompanying documentation.

- `bundler:` – Lists all files that are part of the `bundler` gem. (Don't forget the trailing colon.)

- `bundler:README.md` – View the `README.md` file from the `bundler` gem.

If you don't give the `ri` utility a query as an argument it will enter interactive mode, prompting you for a query. This allows you to input partial names and have them automatically completed when you press the Tab key, along with some other tricks. For more information about the RI tool you can read its documentation by typing the following into a terminal window:

```
ri --help
```

The final tool we'll explore is RDoc, a utility for automatically generating the files that are used by RI. It does this by extracting documentation from Ruby source files written using special formatting rules within code comments. The formatting rules are easy to understand so let's jump right in by looking at a class with a small bit of documentation:

```
# Represents a version number with three components:
#
# * Major number: (1 in +1.2.3+)
# * Minor number: (2 in +1.2.3+)
# * Patch level: (3 in +1.2.3+)
#
```

```
# Example:
#    v = Version.new("10.9.16")
#    v.major # => 10
class Version
  ...
end
```

Documenting something in your Ruby code is as simple as preceding it with a comment. The formatting rules are so unobtrusive that it's both easy to read the documentation directly in the source code and simple to understand how the formatting is converted for RI. You can see that "*" can be used for bullet points in lists but what other formatting rules can you spot? An interesting one is the use of "+" to surround words that should be displayed in a monospaced font. You might have also noticed that the code in the example section of the documentation is indented to the right. This tells RDoc that the entire indented block of text should be displayed as code in a monospaced font. Here's another example, this time documenting a method:

```
# Parses the given version string and creates
# a new Version object.
def initialize (version)
  ...
end
```

You can use all the same formatting rules for methods that you can with class definitions. An interesting thing about the `initialize` method is that it's a private instance method that isn't invoked directly by users of the class. When RDoc parses the comments for `initialize` it will export them as the documentation for the new class method instead. In other words, `initialize` doesn't show up in the documentation for the class, only `new` does.

The style of formatting that we've seen so far is known as—not surprisingly—the RDoc format. There are a handful of other RDoc special characters you can use to style your documentation, all of which are documented in the `RDoc::Markup` class (which you can read with RI). But the RDoc format isn't the only one available. For example, RDoc can also parse documentation written in the Markdown format. While Markdown is becoming ubiquitous for all sorts of writing (including this book) most Ruby documentation is still written in RDoc format. I would venture to say that most Ruby programmers are still expecting to find RDoc formatted comments in Ruby source code (at least for the time being).

Once you've written documentation into your source code it's time to use the `rdoc` utility to extract it. Since we've been focusing on reading documentation in RI let's start by generating files that it can read. Open a terminal window and get yourself into the directory where your project files live. Then type the following command:

```
rdoc -f ri
```

This will recursively scan the current directory for any Ruby source files and build RI documentation for all of them. After it finishes, the files it produced will be in the "doc" directory. You can tell the ri utility to look in this directory for documentation files with the -d command-line option (e.g., "ri -d doc") or ask rdoc to automatically install the generated documentation into a central location using the -r command-line option (e.g., "rdoc -rf ri").

In addition to generating documentation for RI, RDoc can also generate HTML files. This is perfect for reading with a web browser and publishing the documentation somewhere on the web. The -f command-line option to rdoc specifies which formatting engine to use. At the time of writing, RDoc ships with an HTML engine known as *darkfish*. To generate HTML files run this command instead of the previous:

```
rdoc -f darkfish
```

The generated HTML files will be placed in the "doc" directory. The entry point to the documentation is the "index.html" file. As with the ri utility, a lot more information can be found by running rdoc with the --help command-line option. Now go and make the world a better place by documenting your code!

Things to Remember

✦ The ri utility is used for reading documentation and the rdoc utility is used for generating it.

✦ Use the "-d doc" command-line option with the ri utility to have it look in the "doc" directory for documentation.

✦ Generate documentation to be used with RI by running rdoc with the "-f ri" command-line option. Alternatively, use "-f darkfish" to generate HTML.

✦ Complete documentation for the RDoc formatting rules can be found in the RDoc::Markup class (which you can read with RI).

Item 41: Be Aware of IRB's Advanced Features

For many programmers, their very first exposure to Ruby was through the interactive Ruby shell known as IRB. I'm willing to bet yours was too. It's not uncommon for programming languages to have a read-eval-print loop (REPL) utility. These incredibly useful tools turn the programming language into an interactive exploration environment, a place to experiment with language features and libraries. Ruby has an exceptionally wonderful REPL, which provides a playground for novice and expert programmers alike. But many Ruby developers never go beyond that initial encounter with IRB to discover its many advanced features. That's something I'm hoping to rectify here.

Over the next few pages I'll introduce you to helpful IRB features and ways to customize it. The entry point for any customization to IRB is through the IRB configuration file. IRB expects this file to be in your home directory in a file named ".irbrc". (Notice that the file name begins with a period.) Alternatively, you can put the file anywhere you want and then store its location in the IRBRC environment variable. Use whichever method works best on your operating system.

The IRB configuration file is a plain old Ruby source file where you can do anything you'd normally do in Ruby. Changing various IRB settings is done through the IRB.conf method. It returns an internal hash you can modify to change IRB's behavior. For example, you can make IRB automatically indent code entered interactively by setting the :AUTO_INDENT option to true:

```
IRB.conf[:AUTO_INDENT] = true
```

A full list of IRB's configuration options is included in its documentation. You can use these options to customize the command prompt, control how many items are kept in the command history, and even enable Tab key completion. Since this item is concerned with the more advanced features of IRB I won't discuss these simple configuration options any further.

When working inside an IRB session everything you enter will be passed to the Ruby interpreter and evaluated. Even IRB commands—which resemble commands that you enter into a terminal window—turn out to be nothing more than Ruby methods. That's a good thing because it means we can define our own IRB commands by defining methods. For example, let's say we want to write an IRB command called time that can execute a block and then report how many seconds it took to run. One way to accomplish this is by adding an instance method to the Object class. Since IRB evaluates input in an anonymous object by default, our time method would appear to be a top-level command in IRB. But this command would also become a method on *every* object in the current IRB session. That's a bit messy. A better way is to exploit a trick from IRB itself.

The anonymous object where all input is evaluated extends the IRB::ExtendCommandBundle module. If you define an instance method inside that module it will be available as an IRB command without having to infect the Object class. (You could also define instance methods in another module and then include that module into IRB::ExtendCommandBundle. This would be more practical if you were writing a plug-in for IRB.) With that technique in mind, here's an example definition of the time command you could put into your IRB configuration file:

```
module IRB::ExtendCommandBundle
  def time (&block)
   t1 = Time.now
   result = block.call if block
   diff = Time.now - t1
   puts("Time: " + diff.to_f.to_s)
   result
  end
end
```

Besides defining your own commands there are some really nifty IRB tricks you may have missed. The one everyone wishes they knew earlier is the underscore ("_") variable feature. After evaluating input, IRB stores the result of the executed expression in a variable named "_". This is great if you forget to assign the expression to a variable:

```
irb> [1, 2, 3].pop
---> 3

irb> last_elem = _
---> 3
```

Another useful feature in IRB is *sessions*. You can think of sessions as being a way to start a new copy of IRB from within IRB. Each new session in IRB has its own evaluation context; you can set local variables in one session and they won't affect another. But what really makes sessions useful is that you can zoom into any object, making it the current evaluation context and effectively changing the object self references. When working inside IRB, the irb command can be used to create a new session. If given an object as an argument, the irb command will start a new session and make that object the new evaluation context (the self variable):

```
irb> self.class
---> Object

irb> irb [1,2,3]

irb#1> self.class
-----> Array
```

```
irb#1> length
-----> 3
```

Each session in IRB has a unique ID that allows you to manage all of the running sessions from within IRB. You can use the jobs command to list all of the sessions along with their assigned IDs. When given an ID, the fg command will make the session with a matching ID the active session. When you're finished with a session you can use the exit command to terminate the active session or the kill command to terminate a session with a specific ID. There's more to IRB sessions than what I have space for here, including another layer called workspaces, but you can find out more in the documentation for IRB. It can be found in the IRB module, which is part of the Ruby standard library.

One of IRB's greatest strengths is that it's part of Ruby. It's also fairly easy to leverage the IRB library to build your own custom interactive developer tools—the Ruby on Rails console application being a perfect example. And as we've seen, it's possible to extend IRB with new features. Over the years many plug-ins have been written for IRB to add features such as syntax highlighting and improved pretty printers. Unfortunately, most of them have suffered from bit rot and haven't been updated to work with modern versions of Ruby.

If you're looking for something fancier than IRB you may want to consider another popular REPL for Ruby: Pry. This RubyGem has been exploding in popularity over the last couple of years due to its impressive feature list. Out of the box it matches and exceeds IRB in features. It also has a growing repository of plug-ins that adds to Pry's already long list of capabilities. When you're ready to try an alternative to IRB, Pry is just a gem install away.

Things to Remember

◆ Define custom IRB commands in the IRB::ExtendCommandBundle module or a module that is then included into IRB::ExtendCommand Bundle.

◆ Use the underscore ("_") variable to access the result of the last expression.

◆ The irb command can be used to start a new session and change the current evaluation context to an arbitrary object.

◆ Consider the popular Pry gem as an alternative to IRB.

Item 42: Manage Gem Dependencies with Bundler

Newcomers to Ruby often marvel at the incredible number of libraries that are available as RubyGems. If you're looking to add a new feature to one of your applications, you should start by searching the collection of available gems. It's highly likely that someone has already done most of the legwork for you and released their code as a Ruby-Gem. As the saying goes: "There's a gem for that."

As you know, introducing a gem to a new or existing Ruby project is very easy. It usually involves executing the `gem` utility to install the desired library on your development machine followed by an appropriate `require` line somewhere in your project. There's even a built-in way to ask Ruby to only load a specific version of a gem, in case you happen to have multiple versions installed. The `Kernel#gem` method takes the name of a gem and a version specification. It then ensures that a successive call to `require` will only load the correct version of the requested gem. This is a fairly low-level way to manage project dependencies. If it worked for anything other than the most trivial of Ruby projects there wouldn't be anything else to read in this item. But I'm sure you know better than that.

Managing your gems manually is troublesome because it's not easy to keep track of all your dependencies in a reproducible manner. Your project might rely on a handful of gems, and in turn, those gems might have dependencies on other gems, and so forth and so on. Trying to manage the dependency graph manually with the `Kernel#gem` method quickly gets out of hand, especially when you need to install specific versions of these gems on more than one machine. Thankfully, we have the Bundler gem to help us.

Bundler automatically manages the gem-dependency graph and ensures that the exact set of gems you use during development is also used by all other developers and on production servers as well. You specify the gems you need in a file named `Gemfile`. When instructed, Bundler will install all of the necessary gems and their dependencies. It also creates or updates a file named `Gemfile.lock`, which contains the entire dependency graph. It's this file—in conjunction with a source-code version control system—that allows you to reproduce any version of your application along with its exact dependencies.

If you've used a large application framework such as Ruby on Rails you're already familiar with how to use Bundler, at least partially. Rails handles a lot of the Bundler interaction behind the scenes for you. If you haven't used Bundler outside of something like Rails then you might not be aware of how to integrate it into a non-Rails application. That's where this item comes in.

To demonstrate using Bundler in a regular, everyday Ruby project, let's peek at the important parts of a small program that uses a couple of gems. Suppose you'd like to extract the metadata from an MP3 audio file and print it out in the JSON format. The metadata in an MP3 file is stored in the ID3 tag format, so the first thing we're going to need is a RubyGem that can work with MP3 files and ID3 data. Ruby already comes with a JSON library, but to ensure we're working with the latest version we'll also add it as a gem dependency. The very first step when starting out with Bundler is to install the `bundler` RubyGem. Just as with any other gem, Bundler is installed by opening a terminal window and running:

```
gem install bundler
```

Bundler comes with a library named `bundler` and a command-line utility named `bundle`. The utility can be used to create a default `Gemfile`, which is what we'll do now. From a terminal window run the following command:

```
bundle init
```

If you open the newly generated `Gemfile` you'll quickly notice that it's nothing more than a regular Ruby file and is mostly made up of comments. The only actual working line in the entire file looks something like this:

```
source("https://rubygems.org")
```

The `source` method in a `Gemfile` tells Bundler which repository of RubyGems you want to use. The URL in the default `Gemfile` is the official repository and the one you'll most likely want to use. You can list as many gem repositories as you want by including additional `source` lines. This can be helpful if you want to run your own repository for private gems or as a mirror of the official repository. After telling Bundler which repositories you want to use you'll, of course, want to list the gems you're interested in. Suppose that for this simple ID3 to JSON converter you've decided to use the `id3tag` and `json` gems.

When specifying gems in a `Gemfile` you have a lot of options for indicating which versions of those gems you're willing to accept. The `gem` method is used to add a dependency on an external library and has only one mandatory argument: the name of the gem. If the `gem` method is used without any additional details besides the name of the requested gem then Bundler will select the newest version of that gem. This is generally a bad idea because the next time you ask Bundler to update your gems you could potentially end up with newer versions of everything in your `Gemfile`. This may inadvertently introduce breaking changes to your application. You're better off specifying an explicit version (or a range of versions). For now, we'll stick with specific versions of our gems, but in Item 43 we'll focus on safe ways to loosen the version requirements for dependencies. Adding the two gems we've selected for this project to the Gemfile is as simple as adding these two lines:

```
gem('id3tag', '0.7.0')
gem('json',   '1.8.1')
```

After adding gems to the Gemfile you need to tell Bundler to install those gems along with all of their dependencies. This is where we turn back to the bundle command-line utility. To install any missing gems open a terminal window and run the following command:

```
bundle install
```

In addition to installing any necessary gems, the bundle install command will generate a new Gemfile.lock file that includes every gem in the Gemfile as well as all their dependencies. Each gem is listed along with its exact version number. If the Gemfile.lock file exists when you execute bundle install then it will consider the version numbers listed in that file and only install those gem versions. As mentioned earlier, this ensures that your teammates and production servers will be using the same gem versions that you are. (If you want to upgrade a gem to a new version you'll need to update the version number in the Gemfile and then run bundle update. There's more about this in Item 43.)

Now you're ready to use the gems specified in the Gemfile from within the application. There are two ways to do this depending on how much control you want over the process. Let's start with the option that gives us the most flexibility and is the most familiar. All you have to do is require the "bundler/setup" file and then require the other gems like normal:

```
require('bundler/setup')
require('id3tag')
require('json')
```

Loading the "bundler/setup" file alters the environment your program is running in so that Ruby can find the gems we need without accidentally finding gems that haven't been listed in the Gemfile. This includes restricting the gems to those specified in the Gemfile.lock file. After loading Bundler you're free to require the other gems as you need them, all at once or sprinkled throughout the source of the program. Of course, if your Gemfile has *a lot* of gems then requiring each gem in your program can be a bit painful and will introduce some duplication. In that case, you have another option—ask Bundler to load all of the gems for you:

```
require('bundler/setup')
Bundler.require
```

Placing these two lines in your program will cause it to load Bundler and then every gem defined in the Gemfile. More specifically, when the Bundler::require method is called without any arguments it will load all of the gems in the Gemfile. But you can give it one or more names of a *gem group* and then Bundler will only load the gems that are part of those groups. You can define groups in the Gemfile by using the group method:

```
group(:production) do
  gem('id3tag', '0.7.0')
  gem('json',   '1.8.1')
end
```

Groups can be useful when you want to create environments where some gems are used and others are not. For example, it's fairly common to create a test group where you list all of your testing gems. You can then instruct Bundler to install those gems on your development machines but not on the production servers. (For more information about deploying specific groups to your production servers see the documentation for Bundler.) Changing our program to only load the gems in the production group is pretty straightforward:

```
require('bundler/setup')
Bundler.require(:production)
```

Up to this point Bundler has been used to manage the dependencies for a program that you're not planning on distributing. But being the warm, caring person that you are, you'll probably want to share some of your code with the Ruby community at some point. When you do, the most accepted way is by wrapping that code up into a gem. You'll still be able to use Bundler to help you manage the dependencies of your gem but things are a little bit different here. Let's take a short look at how to use Bundler to develop a RubyGem.

Earlier, when we wanted to create a default Gemfile, we used the bundle init command. To package your code as a RubyGem you're going to need a few more files. Thankfully, the bundle utility can also generate a skeleton project that is ready for packaging and distribution. You need to give Bundler a name for your new project so for this example let's say you decided to use "mp3json". From a terminal window run the following command:

```
bundle gem mp3json
```

This will instruct Bundler to create an mp3json directory and fill it with all sorts of useful files, including some source files to help get you started. Since we're focusing on Bundler, the two files we're interested in are mp3json.gemspec and Gemfile. Let's start with the familiar Gemfile. This time Bundler generated one that looks slightly different than what we're used to:

```
source('https://rubygems.org')

gemspec
```

The line containing an invocation of the source method should be familiar, but what's that gemspec method do? To create a package for your code the RubyGems system needs information about your gem, including its dependencies. All the details about your gem are written into a specification file; in our case it's that mp3json.gemspec file I mentioned earlier. To avoid duplicating information, Bundler allows you to keep your dependencies in the gem-specification file where they belong and use the gemspec method in your Gemfile to pretend they're in the Gemfile too. This means that during development you can continue to use the bundle install command to install dependencies. In the gem-specification file you use the Gem::Specification::new method to specify all the details about your gem such as its name, version number, description, etc. How to specify those fields is obvious once you open the generated gem-specification file, but what's not so obvious is how to add dependencies on other gems. Here's an example using the gems from the MP3/ID3 project:

```
Gem::Specification.new do |gem|
  gem.add_dependency('id3tag', '0.7.0')
  gem.add_dependency('json',   '1.8.1')
  ...
end
```

The Gem::Specification#add_dependency method is a lot like the gem method available in a Gemfile. The only required argument is the name of the gem you want to add as a dependency. But like before, we'll give an explicit version number to make installing our gem a bit more predictable. (In reality, you'll probably want to loosen this restriction a bit; see Item 43 for more details.)

A final word of caution: When writing an application, it's important to place the Gemfile.lock file in your version-control system. This file allows you to ensure that deployments to production include the exact same gems that were used in development. But the same is not true when writing a library to be distributed as a RubyGem. In that case, the general recommendation is to *not* include the Gemfile.lock file in your version-control system. Doing so complicates the development process for a gem and keeps you from noticing incompatibilities between your gem and its dependencies.

Things to Remember

+ In exchange for a little bit of flexibility you can load all of the gems specified in your Gemfile by using Bundler.require after loading Bundler.

+ When developing an application, list your gems in the Gemfile and add the Gemfile.lock file to your version-control system.

+ When developing a RubyGem, list your gem dependencies in the gem-specification file and do *not* include the Gemfile.lock file in your version-control system.

Item 43: Specify an Upper Bound for Gem Dependencies

There are a few different ways to introduce a gem as a dependency in your project. In Item 42 we looked at these three methods: using Ruby-Gems directly in your source code with the gem method, using Bundler to list dependencies in a Gemfile, and using the add_dependency method in a gem specification. All three of these methods allow you to place restrictions on gems based on something called a *gem requirement*. This basically boils down to specifying a range of version numbers that your project is known to work with. Here's something you're likely to see in a Bundler Gemfile out in the wild:

```
gem('money', '>= 1.0')
```

This line adds a dependency on the money gem with a requirement that Bundler selects at least version 1.0. Specifying a lower bound on the gem requirement without an upper bound means that you'll accept the version listed and all future versions. Even though this is really common, it's a recipe for disaster. Can you really say that your application will work with every future version of a gem? Of course not. But the harm might not be immediately obvious, especially since we have the Gemfile.lock file to protect us, right? Not quite.

Suppose you're in charge of the maintenance for an application that is a few years old. All of the gems in the Gemfile have version requirements that only contain lower bounds, no upper bounds. Following the advice in Item 42, you've committed the Gemfile.lock file to your source code control system. Now, let's say you've spent a long night debugging this application and have tracked a problem down to one of the gems. You do some poking around and discover that the author of the buggy gem has released a new version that fixes the problem you're seeing. In your excitement (and lack of sleep) you ask Bundler to update your gems by running the following command:

```
bundle update
```

Boom! All of your tests start failing. Guess what...you just updated all of your gems to their latest versions and some of them contained changes that are not backward compatible. If you didn't have your Gemfile.lock under version control you'd be in a world of hurt because Bundler also just updated it with all the latest version numbers. There are two ways to prevent something like this from happening. One really simple way is to make sure you only update one gem at a time. Bundler can be smart about introducing just a single update to the dependency graph by telling the bundle utility which gem you want to upgrade:

```
bundle update money
```

This will only get you so far. If you're packaging a library as a Ruby-Gem you need to list the version requirements for your gem's dependencies in the gem-specification file. In this situation you won't have control over the Gemfile being used by other programmers. Without an upper bound on your gem's dependencies it might break for others when one of these dependencies introduces a breaking change. You can't predict the future and omitting an upper bound on version requirements, whether in your Gemfile or somewhere else, is akin to saying that you can. To fix this, let's explore the process of managing version requirements using explicit version numbers and how to introduce flexibility with a range of version numbers.

When developing an application your best bet is to manage your dependencies with Bundler and a Gemfile. Personally, I like to specify my gems with an explicit version like this:

```
gem('money', '5.1.1')
```

This way you share in the responsibility of managing gems. You're in charge of maintaining the explicit version requirements for your direct dependencies and Bundler uses the Gemfile.lock file to maintain the dependencies of those gems. No gem can get updated without someone updating a version requirement in the Gemfile. Some people consider this a bit strict. If you'd like more flexibility you can specify a version range by giving more than one requirement:

```
gem('money', '>= 5.1.0', '< 5.2.0')
```

Specifying a range like this has become so common that there's even a custom operator that offers a shortcut: the pessimistic version operator. It might look a bit strange at first but the previous version range can be expressed with the pessimistic version operator like this:

```
gem('money', '~> 5.1.0')
```

The pessimistic version operator creates a range of version numbers by manipulating the version string to its right. In this example, the lower bound of the range turns into ">= 5.1.0". The upper bound is created in two steps. First, the rightmost digit is removed from the version string, so 5.1.0 becomes 5.1. Next, the new rightmost digit is incremented, changing 5.1 into 5.2. The resulting number becomes the upper bound: "< 5.2.0". This sort of "fuzzy" behavior can be a little confusing so I prefer explicit lower and upper bounds to using the pessimistic version operator. And since the pessimistic version operator can't express more detailed ranges it's not really appropriate for our next task—specifying dependencies when writing a library.

Recall that when developing a RubyGem you use the add_dependency method in a gem-specification file to add a dependency on another gem. When someone installs your gem they'll automatically download and install all of its dependencies. I mentioned earlier that I prefer explicit gem versions, but that doesn't work at all in this scenario. An example might be helpful.

Suppose you're writing a gem that can fetch stock quotes and calculate rates of return. Naturally, you'll want to use the money gem because doing arithmetic with money can be a bit goofy and the money gem is well established and tested. Let's say you put the following in your gem specification:

```
Gem::Specification.new do |gem|
  gem.add_dependency('money', '4.2.0')
  ...
end
```

You've fully tested your gem against version 4.2.0 of the money gem so that's the version requirement you put in the gem specification. Continuing along with this example, suppose that somebody is writing an application to produce pretty return on investment charts and they want to use your nifty gem. They're already using the money gem, except they need features that were introduced in version 5.0. See the problem? The person writing this charting app can't use your gem because their application would require two different versions of the money gem, and that's not allowed.

If you're going to release a gem to the public and it has dependencies on other gems, you have a responsibility of sorts to provide a flexible range of versions for those dependencies. The lower bound is easy— pick the earliest version of the dependency that you know to work correctly with your package. The upper bound is a little trickier because you have a few different choices. Going against the advice in this item, you can simply omit the upper bound. But that's not very nice to the community because you have no way of knowing that your gem is going to continue to work for all future versions of its dependencies. The right thing to do is to supply a reasonable upper bound. This can either be the last known working version of the dependency or even a bit more flexible and up to (but not including) the next major release.

Let's say you know your gem works with version 4.2.0 of the money gem, and you've also tested it with version 5.1.1. You have reason to expect that the author of the money gem won't introduce any breaking changes without changing the version number to 5.2.0 and so conclude that all of the 5.1.x releases will be safe. This allows you to write a much more flexible gem specification:

```
Gem::Specification.new do |gem|
  gem.add_dependency('money', '>= 4.2.0', '< 5.2.0')
  ...
end
```

This wider range of version requirements makes your gem flexible enough to work with past and future versions of the money gem without taking on too much risk of breakage. It also means you don't have to release a new version of your gem each time the developer of the money gem releases a small patch version. I'd say that's a good compromise.

Things to Remember

+ Omitting an upper bound on a version requirement is akin to saying that your application or library supports all future versions of a dependency.

+ Prefer an explicit range of version numbers over the pessimistic version operator.

+ When releasing a gem to the public, specify the dependency version requirement as wide as you safely can with an upper bound that extends until the next potentially breaking release.

Memory Management and Performance

There's an old elevator pitch that proclaims that Ruby improves programmer happiness and therefore makes programmers more productive. Or you may have heard it this way: "Ruby is optimized for programmer performance." Either way, I think there's some truth in those statements. In that light, you can consider this book to be a guide for improving your happiness with Ruby. That is, excluding this chapter.

You can write code all day long with a smile on your face but eventually your application is going to have to execute in the real world. Once that happens you're going to hobble along until you realize that parts of your application will need to run faster or with less memory. In Ruby, these two things are often directly related.

Figuring out why your application is performing poorly isn't always an easy task. Knowing which tools to use is only one part of the solution. Knowing how Ruby manages memory and how you can reduce the number of garbage-collection cycles is another. This chapter opens with an in-depth look at the garbage collector: how it works and how to adjust its performance.

The remainder of the chapter is dedicated to helping you track down performance issues with tips for fixing them. Maybe when you're done you can put that smile back on your face and find joy in writing optimized Ruby code.

Item 44: Familiarize Yourself with Ruby's Garbage Collector

A running Ruby program is made up of objects and lots of them. For example, kicking off a fresh copy of IRB allocates around 100k objects before the garbage collector prunes that number down to roughly 12k active objects. Practically everything you do in Ruby requires memory in one way or another. Managing all that manually would be tedious and error-prone, but thankfully, we don't have to.

The job of the garbage collector is to manage a pool of memory and eventually release objects that are no longer being used. Since every computer has a finite amount of memory, it's advantageous to free up these unused objects. While we don't have to manage memory manually since we have a garbage collector, we do have to give up a bit of performance for it. For the garbage collector to do its job properly it needs to pause your program while it's running. Every major release of Ruby has included improvements to the garbage collector, most aimed at reducing the amount of time that program execution needs to be halted. There are also ways to tune the garbage collector to improve its performance for a specific application's performance profile. But let's not get ahead of ourselves.

Before we dive into tuning and exploiting the garbage collector let's see how it works. Garbage collectors are complicated pieces of software engineering and come in several variations. From a very high level Ruby's garbage collector uses a process called *mark and sweep,* which is made up of two phases. First, the object graph is traversed. Objects that are still reachable from your code are considered alive and subsequently *marked.* Next, any objects that weren't marked in the first phase are considered garbage and are *swept* away, releasing their memory back to Ruby and possibly the operating system.

Traversing the object graph and marking reachable objects is expensive. Ruby 2.1 introduced an optimization through a new generational garbage collector. Objects are divided into two categories: young and old. Generational garbage collectors work from the premise that most objects don't live very long. So, if an object survives for enough time it can be assumed that it's likely to continue living even longer. There are lots of objects like this in any Ruby program, one category being those referenced from constants. Knowing that an object is likely to survive for a long time means the garbage collector can optimize the mark phase by automatically marking old objects as reachable, skipping entire sections of the object graph while traversing.

Ruby's generational garbage collector promotes young objects to old objects if they survive one marking phase. That is, they lived long enough to still be reachable since the garbage collector was last triggered. With the concept of young and old objects, the marking phase can be split into two modes: *major* and *minor.* During the major marking phase all objects (young and old) are considered for marking. In this mode, the garbage collector doesn't consider generations and is therefore more expensive. Minor marking, on the other hand, only considers young objects and automatically marks old objects without checking to see if they're still reachable. This means that old objects can only be swept away after a major marking phase. The garbage collector prefers to use minor marking unless some thresholds have been met to warrant a full, major marking. We'll dig deeper into these thresholds shortly.

The sweeping phase of the garbage collector also has an optimization that divides it into two modes: *immediate* and *lazy*. In the immediate mode, the garbage collector will free all unmarked objects. If there are a lot of objects to release then this mode will be expensive. So, the sweeping phase also supports a lazy mode where it will attempt to free the minimum number of objects possible. Each time you create a new object in Ruby it might trigger a lazy sweeping phase to free up some space. To better understand this we need to look at how the garbage collector manages the memory where objects are stored.

Depending on the operating system it can be expensive for an application to request a memory allocation from the free store. A common workaround is to allocate more memory than you immediately need and maintain a memory pool, only asking the operating system for additional memory when the pool is empty. This is the technique the Ruby garbage collector uses. Ruby's pool of memory is known as the *heap* (not to be confused with the operating system's free store, which is sometimes referred to as the heap). Ruby's heap is divided into *pages*, which are subdivided into *slots*. Each slot is used to hold a single Ruby object. Figure 8-1 shows an example of the Ruby heap before and after garbage collection.

When a Ruby application first starts it will allocate several pages and place them in the heap. As I mentioned before, when you create an object, the garbage collector will first look for an empty slot in which

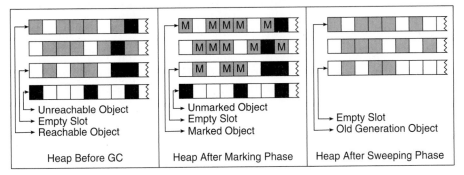

Figure 8-1 Marking and sweeping pages in the heap.

to store the new object. If one can't be found it will attempt a lazy sweeping phase in order to free one. If it still can't find an empty slot the garbage collector will allocate a new page and add it to the heap. During a sweeping phase, if all slots in a page are released, the garbage collector might decide to return that page back to the operating system's free store. This means that, as observed from the viewpoint of the operating system, the memory footprint of a Ruby process will appear to grow and shrink over time. From the inside, a Ruby process grows and shrinks by pages and not individual objects.

The number of initial slots can have an effect on the time it takes to start a Ruby program. (Think about all those classes and modules that are getting created as your source code and all of its dependencies are loaded. If it exceeds the number of available slots the garbage collector will have to allocate more pages, which might incur a performance penalty.) The default number of slots is likely to change between Ruby versions. With that in mind, the number of initial slots in Ruby 2.1 is 10k. The number of slots per page in the same version is 408. With those two numbers we can calculate that Ruby will allocate 24 pages on boot (the number of pages is rounded down to the nearest integer). You can change the number of initial slots (and thus the initial number of pages) by setting the RUBY_GC_HEAP_INIT_SLOTS environment variable. There are a few other environment variables that can be used to tune the garbage collector—we'll walk through those in a moment. But first, I want to show you how to access garbage collector statistics. Start an IRB session and run the following code:

```
irb> GC.stat
---> {:count=>9, :heap_length=>126, ...}
```

The GC::stat method will return a hash containing all sorts of interesting information about the garbage collector. Keep in mind that the keys in this hash and what they mean are internal to the garbage collector and may change in the next Ruby version. That said...let's take a look at some of the more interesting keys:

- count, major_gc_count, and minor_gc_count tell you how many times the garbage collector has run in total, in major mode, and in minor mode, respectively.

- total_allocated_object and total_freed_object are the total number of objects created since the Ruby program began and the number of objects released. The difference between the two is the number of live objects, which can be found through the heap_live_slot key.

- `heap_length` is the number of pages currently in the heap.

- `heap_live_slot` and `heap_free_slot` are the number of used and available slots across all pages.

- `old_object` is the number of objects that are in the old generation and won't be processed by a minor marking phase. The difference between `heap_live_slot` and `old_object` will tell you the number of young objects.

There are a couple of other interesting numbers in that hash, but before we review them it's important to understand one final thing about the garbage collector. Recall that objects are stored in slots. The size of a slot in Ruby 2.1 is 40 bytes. Of course, not all objects can fit within that space. For example, consider a string containing 255 characters. When an object needs more memory than is available in its slot space, Ruby requests a chunk of memory from the operating system's free store. When the object is destroyed and its slot is freed, Ruby will return the extra memory to the operating system. Now let's look at a few more entries from the `GC::stat` hash:

- `malloc_increase` is the total number of bytes being used by objects that need more memory than is available in their slots.

- `malloc_limit` is a threshold value. If the value of `malloc_increase` exceeds `malloc_limit` the garbage collector will run in minor mode. The value of `malloc_limit` is adjusted dynamically during the life of a Ruby program by multiplying the current value of `malloc_increase` by an adjustable factor whose default value is 1.4. You can change the factor by setting the `RUBY_GC_MALLOC_LIMIT_GROWTH_FACTOR` environment variable.

- `oldmalloc_increase` and `oldmalloc_limit` are the old generation counterparts of `malloc_increase` and `malloc_limit`. When `oldmalloc_increase` exceeds `oldmalloc_limit` the garbage collector runs in major mode. The default multiplier for `oldmalloc_limit` is 1.2 and can be changed with the `RUBY_GC_OLDMALLOC_LIMIT_GROWTH_FACTOR` environment variable.

Let's wrap up by reviewing the environment variables that can be used to tune the garbage collector for a specific application. Just as with the values in the `GC::stat` hash, these environment variables might change in the next Ruby release. As a matter of fact, there's a good chance that Ruby 2.2 will support three generations as opposed to two. That will probably have an impact on these settings. The definitive source for information on tuning the garbage collector with environment variables can be found in the "gc.c" file, which is part of

the Ruby source code. Here are the settings that can be changed in
Ruby 2.1:

- RUBY_GC_HEAP_INIT_SLOTS: The number of initial slots to create.
  Increasing this number from its default of 10k can reduce the
  number of times the garbage collector runs while your application
  is booting.

- RUBY_GC_HEAP_FREE_SLOTS: The minimum number of slots that
  should be available after the garbage collector runs. If the number
  of free slots drops below this value then additional pages will be
  allocated and added to the heap. The default value is 4096.

- RUBY_GC_HEAP_GROWTH_FACTOR: A multiplier that is used to decide how
  many pages should be added to the heap when adding additional
  slots. The number of used pages is multiplied by this factor to determine the number of pages to grow to. The default value is 1.8.

- RUBY_GC_HEAP_GROWTH_MAX_SLOTS: The maximum number of slots
  that can be added to the heap in one allocation. The default value
  is 0, which disables an upper limit.

- RUBY_GC_HEAP_OLDOBJECT_LIMIT_FACTOR: A multiplier used to calculate a threshold that when exceeded will force a major garbage collection. The threshold is calculated by multiplying this factor by
  the number of old objects from the last major garbage collection.
  The threshold is compared to the current number of old objects.
  The default value is 2.0, which means that if the number of old
  objects doubles since the last major marking phase another major
  marking will be forced.

- RUBY_GC_MALLOC_LIMIT: The minimum value for the malloc_limit
  key from the GC::stat hash. If the malloc_increase value exceeds
  malloc_limit a minor garbage collection is triggered. This setting keeps malloc_increase from going below a specific value. The
  default value is 16,777,216 (16MB).

- RUBY_GC_MALLOC_LIMIT_MAX: This is the opposite of the
  RUBY_GC_MALLOC_LIMIT setting that keeps the malloc_limit value
  from going too high. It can be set to 0 to remove an upper limit.
  The default value is 33,554,432 (32MB).

- RUBY_GC_MALLOC_LIMIT_GROWTH_FACTOR: A multiplier that controls
  how the malloc_limit value grows over time. A new malloc_limit
  value is calculated by multiplying this factor by the current value
  of malloc_limit. The default value is 1.4.

- RUBY_GC_OLDMALLOC_LIMIT: The old-generation counterpart of
  RUBY_GC_MALLOC_LIMIT. The default value is 16,777,216 (16MB).

- RUBY_GC_OLDMALLOC_LIMIT_MAX: The old-generation counterpart of RUBY_GC_MALLOC_LIMIT_MAX. The default value is 134,217,728 (128MB).

- RUBY_GC_OLDMALLOC_LIMIT_GROWTH_FACTOR: The old-generation counterpart of RUBY_GC_MALLOC_LIMIT_GROWTH_FACTOR. The default value is 1.2.

Armed with these settings you should be able to decrease the time it takes to boot your application. But that's just the beginning. The garbage collector gives you enough tuning knobs to reduce the number of times it becomes active during your application. Minimizing the number of times the garbage collector runs can directly influence the performance of your application, especially if you have plenty of memory to spare.

Things to Remember

- ✦ The garbage collector manages memory by maintaining a heap composed of pages that are subdivided into slots. One slot can house one object.

- ✦ During garbage collection, reachable objects are marked and unmarked objects are swept away, opening slots for new objects.

- ✦ New objects are called *young* and are promoted to being *old* if they survive one cycle of the garbage collector. Old objects are automatically marked as being active in minor marking phases and therefore can only be swept away after major marking phases.

- ✦ The GC::stat method returns statistics about the garbage collector in the form of a hash.

- ✦ You can tune the garbage collector for your specific application by setting environment variables.

Item 45: Create Resource Safety Nets with Finalizers

Back in Item 24 we looked at how to use ensure clauses to release resources, even in the presence of exceptions. That item also explored a pattern where a class method allocates a resource, passes it to a block, and then releases the resource. The actual act of releasing the resource is done inside an ensure clause so it happens even if the invoked block raises an exception. As a refresher, here's a generic class that manages an internal resource:

```
class Resource
  def self.open (&block)
```

```
    resource = new
    block.call(resource) if block
  ensure
    resource.close if resource
  end
end
```

Unfortunately, there are some specific cases where this pattern can't be used. One example is when you need to hold on to a resource for a period of time longer than which you can spend inside an ensure clause. Most resource classes provide an alternative interface that allows programmers to get around this automatic releasing, leaving the programmer responsible for manually releasing the resource when they are done with it. In this case, you should consider using the garbage collector to ensure that the resource will eventually be released even if the programmer accidentally forgets.

Ruby doesn't have deterministic destructors like a lot of languages do. The closest workaround is to register a finalizer with the garbage collector. Finalizers are Proc objects that are invoked *after* an object has been destroyed. They are very tricky to write correctly so splash some water on your face and pay close attention. The following additions to the Resource class provide an interface programmers can use to manually manage objects, with the added bonus that the garbage collector is used as a safety net:

```
class Resource
  # Manual (dangerous) interface.
  def initialize
    @resource = allocate_resource
    finalizer = self.class.finalizer(@resource)
    ObjectSpace.define_finalizer(self, finalizer)
  end

  def close
    ObjectSpace.undefine_finalizer(self)
    @resource.close
  end

  # Return a Proc which can be used to free a resource.
  def self.finalizer (resource)
    lambda {|id| resource.close}
  end
end
```

First, in order to focus on the important parts, I've omitted a couple of method definitions from this class whose implementations are unimportant. I'll mention what they're for and what you could do with them as they are encountered.

The `initialize` method calls the `allocate_resource` method, which should create and return the actual resource we're protecting. This might be something like a database connection or a handle to a running process. The next step in `initialize` is a bit strange. It uses a class method to create a `Proc` object. This might seem completely unnecessary, but this technique wouldn't work without it. Before I explain, let's look at that final line in the `initialize` method. It uses the `ObjectSpace::define_finalizer` method to tell the garbage collector that after its first argument is destroyed it should invoke the `Proc` object in its second argument. To understand how tricky this method is we need to take a slight detour and talk about the garbage collector and closures.

As I mentioned earlier, finalizers are invoked *after* an object is destroyed. You might remember from Item 44 that the garbage collector will destroy objects after they are no longer reachable from the running program. And due to several optimization rules the garbage collector might take a while to get around to destroying unreachable objects. The thing you need to watch out for is that the `Proc` object that represents the finalizer *must not* hold on to a reference to the object that is doomed to destruction. If it does, then as far as the garbage collector is concerned it's still reachable. Let's explore that further. Pretend that I had written this version of `initialize` instead of the previous:

```ruby
def initialize
  @resource = allocate_resource

  # DON'T DO THIS!!
  finalizer = lambda {|id| @resource.close}
  ObjectSpace.define_finalizer(self, finalizer)
end
```

Recall that creating a `Proc` object also creates a closure, or in other words, a binding where all local variables that existed when the `Proc` was created are usable from within the body of the `Proc`. Here's the catch: This closure also captures the `self` variable. If the finalizer holds on to the `Resource` object this way, the garbage collector will always mark it as being reachable and never remove it from the program. This can happen invisibly by a closure holding on to `self` or directly by referencing self in the body of the Proc. That's why the original version of initialize used a class method to create the Proc—the self variable in that context refers to the class and not the current Resource object.

This can't be overstated. If the Proc used with define_finalizer was created in a binding that can reference the object you're interested in finalizing, the garbage collector *will not* be able to release it. If your finalizers don't appear to run until the program terminates, there's a good chance you've trapped the object in a closure. With that thought hammered into your head, let's close with a couple of tips.

The lambda used as the finalizer's Proc object took a single argument (which it didn't use but *must* accept). A common mistake is to assume that this argument is the object that is being destroyed. While that would actually be pretty nice it's not the case. The argument given to the finalizer is the ID of the recently destroyed object. Not as useful as the object itself but maybe still useful in some situations. You should also know that any exceptions generated from within the finalizer Proc will be ignored.

Notice that the Resource#close method uses undefine_finalizer. If the close method is called then we don't need to close the internal resource a second time from within the finalizer. The safety net is no longer required and can be safely removed. While this simple example doesn't demonstrate it, each object may actually have any number of associated finalizers. That is, you can use define_finalizer any number of times and the garbage collector will keep all of them. Calling ObjectSpace::undefine_finalizer removes all registered finalizers at once. The ObjectSpace API doesn't provide a way to remove a single finalizer—it's all or nothing.

The last thing I want to mention before we wrap up is *timing*. The garbage collector is highly optimized so that it runs as infrequently as possible. It might take some time for an unreachable object to be destroyed. But here's the kicker: Finalizers are a low-priority job for the garbage collector. Finalizers may be called anytime after an object is destroyed and before the program terminates. That's why it's a last ditch effort and the ensure clause approach used in Item 24 is much more ideal.

Things to Remember

✦ Prefer to use ensure clauses to protect limited resources.

✦ If you must expose a resource outside of an ensure clause, create a finalizer for it.

✦ Never create a finalizer Proc within a binding that can reference the object you're interested in finalizing. This will keep the object from being releasable by the garbage collector.

✦ Keep in mind that finalizers may be called anytime after an object is destroyed and before the program terminates.

Item 46: Be Aware of Ruby Profiling Tools

When your code isn't performing quite as well as you'd like it's easy to make assumptions about where there might be bottlenecks. Of course, if you blindly follow these assumptions you can waste a lot of time improving the performance of insignificant inefficiencies. Like everything in life, you should follow the evidence wherever it may lead you and avoid forming conclusions without supporting data. "So, what evidence can I review to improve the performance of my Ruby programs?" I'm glad you asked.

The first step in diagnosing a performance problem is collecting statistics. They should include details such as where your program spends most of its time and which parts use the most amount of memory. The way to collect these statistics is by using a profiling tool. Armed with a performance profile of your program you can adjust problematic sections of the code. You can then generate another profile and compare it with the first to see the impact of your handiwork. We're going to take a look at a few different ways to generate these performance profiles. The profiles I'm about to show you were generated using trivial example code. I'm omitting the code listing so we can focus on how to generate and interpret the profiles since these tasks apply equally to any Ruby program.

The first profiling tool we'll use is built into Ruby and exposed as a standard library. This is a good thing because it means that if you have Ruby installed you automatically have a profiling tool that works with that version of Ruby. To use this built-in tool you can either require the profile library directly from within your source code, or more easily, by asking Ruby to require it for you:

```
ruby -rprofile script.rb
```

If you haven't seen it before, the "-r" command-line option to the ruby executable is exactly the same as using require in your source code. The previous command tells Ruby to require the profile library and then execute the script.rb file. After the file has finished executing (or when you kill the appropriate ruby process) the profile library will print out a performance profile to the terminal. But be warned— loading the profile library will drastically increase the amount of time it takes to execute your program. It might be a bit frustrating but don't worry about the additional execution time; everything is slowed down equally so the performance profile will still be accurate. When the performance profile is finally produced it will look something like this:

% time	cumulative seconds	self seconds	calls	self ms/call	total ms/call	name
62.60	15.70	3.92	433413	0.04	0.16	CSV#shift
10.13	18.24	2.54	14054	0.18	1.58	Array#each
4.39	19.34	1.10	405451	0.00	0.00	String#=~
3.79	20.29	0.95	405472	0.00	0.00	String#[]
3.51	21.17	0.88	420453	0.00	0.00	Hash#[]
3.27	21.99	0.82	405924	0.00	0.00	Array#<<
3.15	22.78	0.79	419475	0.00	0.00	String#==

I've trimmed the output for brevity. It's likely that the actual output is much longer. In this particular example you can see that 62.6% of the execution time is spent on the CSV#shift method. To put that into perspective you first need to consider the other columns in the report.

The "% time," "calls," and "name" columns are obvious. The remaining columns are split into two categories: self and total/cumulative. To understand the difference between the two consider what happens when one method invokes another: When method a calls method b we consider a to be the parent and b to be the child. The "total ms/call" column reports the average number of milliseconds taken by a method per invocation, including the time used by its children. The "self ms/call" column, on the other hand, does not include the execution time associated with a method's children. In the same way, "cumulative seconds" shows the total amount of time a method took for all invocations combined, including the time taken by its children. The "self seconds" column is the same measurement but without the children included.

Looking at the first line again, we can see that CSV#shift spends 75% of its time invoking and waiting for other methods. (You can see this by comparing "total ms/call" and "self ms/call".) Unfortunately, it's not clear which methods those are or even how many there are. This type of profile is known as a *flat* profile and is mostly useful for tracking down the most expensive methods in a program. If you need more information you'll have to turn to other profiling tools, and that's what we'll do now.

A very popular and capable profiling tool is the ruby-prof gem. Besides producing a variety of reports, ruby-prof is also *a lot* faster than the standard profile library that ships with Ruby. It can produce text reports like the profile library, along with HTML reports and call-graph diagrams. Consider this call stack profile that I've adapted from HTML and trimmed for brevity:

```
94.91% CSV#each                  [     1 calls]
-> 93.44% CSV#shift              [ 13982 calls]
   -> 91.27% Kernel#loop         [ 13982 calls]
      |> 9.47% String#=~         [405449 calls]
      |> 8.00% String#[]         [405449 calls]
      |> 5.77% Array#<<          [405449 calls]
      |> 5.72% Hash#[]           [419430 calls]
      |> 5.54% String#empty?     [419430 calls]
      |> 5.40% String#==         [405449 calls]
      |> 2.56% String#split      [ 13981 calls]
      |> 1.20% String#sub!       [ 13981 calls]
```

This profile reports the parent-child relationship between methods by placing the child below and to the right of the parent. We can now see that CSV#shift calls Kernel#loop, which calls several String methods. If you compare this report with the flat profile from earlier you can see that CSV#shift spends most of its time calling String#=~ to match strings against regular expressions.

It's worth noting that the statistics reported by the two profiles we've seen thus far are different. This is an unfortunate artifact of using different tools with different data-collection techniques and performance penalties. I recommend that you prefer the ruby-prof gem to the standard profile library. The former is much faster and produces several different reports, including flat profiles. But if you're using Ruby 2.1, there's another tool you should consider.

Beginning in version 2.1, Ruby includes a tracing and profiling facility that can be used by extensions written in C. The main advantage of this new feature can be found in the fact that it's fast, *very* fast. In my experiments there was no noticeable difference between executing code with and without the new API activated. That's quite impressive as far as profiling goes. At the time of writing, the best way to profile your code using this new API is by using the stackprof gem.

Unlike with the previous profiling tools we've seen, stackprof must be explicitly activated in your code to generate a profile. This is done by requiring the stackprof library and then using StackProf::run. This method takes a block and records profiling information while the block is executing. Here's an example:

```
require("stackprof")
StackProf.run(out: "profile.dump") do
  ...
end
```

After the block has finished, StackProf::run will write a profile report into the file specified by the named argument out. This is a binary file created with the Marshal::dump method. The easiest way to work with this file is through the included stackprof utility. The following command will print out a flat profile report to the terminal:

```
stackprof profile.dump
```

In addition to the flat profile, stackprof can generate a small number of other reports as well, both human-readable and those meant for other tools. Like with ruby-prof, stackprof has good documentation that includes more advanced examples than what I can include here. If you're using Ruby 2.1 or later I highly recommend that you consider using stackprof.

So far we've used three different tools to create performance profiles. The statistics we've collected have illuminated slow methods, methods that were called a large number of times, and how a method's children can influence its performance. What we haven't seen is how to measure the memory use of a program and find out if any of our methods are memory hogs. Unfortunately, memory profiling in Ruby isn't as mature as it should be.

Part of that has to do with the fact that Ruby uses a garbage collector. So, if Ruby manages memory for us, we're kind of stuck with its performance, right? Well, yes *and* no. As you'll see in Item 47, it's not hard to create a lot of temporary objects and slow things down. It's also possible to accidentally keep a reference to an object for longer than you'd like. Doing so can actually lead to a memory leak since the long-lived reference prevents the garbage collector from getting rid of the referenced object.

Another problem with memory profiling is that the Ruby garbage collector and memory-management code is a constantly moving target. As it turns out, there are quite a few memory-profiling gems available, but the vast majority of them only work with older versions of Ruby. The only one that works across all of the Ruby versions supported by this book is a gem we've already seen: ruby-prof. It works around the ever-changing garbage collector by injecting its own memory profiling functionality into the Ruby interpreter. As a consequence, to profile memory with ruby-prof you have to build a custom version of Ruby. If you're using a version of Ruby before 2.1, ruby-prof and a custom Ruby interpreter is your best option. Profiling memory in ruby-prof is done by selecting one of the memory-reporting options with the "--mode" command-line option. Here's an example:

```
ruby-prof --mode=memory script.rb
```

Starting with Ruby 2.1 there's a new, experimental API for collecting memory statistics. There's also a gem that makes it really easy to use this API, but we'll get to that. Ruby exposes two sets of APIs through the GC and ObjectSpace modules. The GC module can be used to control the garbage collector—we've already seen how to use the GC::stat method to see what the garbage collector has been up to. In a similar way, the ObjectSpace module allows you to get quite a bit of information about the large number of objects being managed by Ruby. It also provides an API to collect and record memory-allocation statistics. Here's how you start collecting that information:

```ruby
require("objspace")

# Start collecting allocation information.
ObjectSpace.trace_object_allocations_start
```

Once you've started collecting memory-allocation information you can record it to a file. Depending on your program, you might want to wait until just before it terminates or record the allocation information at regular intervals. Either way, it's a good idea to start by forcing the garbage collector to run so that any unreachable objects are swept away. This should help improve the accuracy of the report and remove irrelevant information. Recording the allocation statistics to a file is easy:

```ruby
# Force garbage collector to run.
GC.start

# Write current statistics to a file.
File.open("memory.json", "w") do |file|
  ObjectSpace.dump_all(output: file)
end
```

If you're collecting memory information through the ObjectSpace API you'll most likely keep the tracing enabled for the duration of your program. But if you want to disable it, you can:

```ruby
# Stop collecting allocation information.
ObjectSpace.trace_object_allocations_stop
```

The file created by the dump_all method can be quite large. As the file name suggests, the data written into it is in the JSON format. While this does make it human-readable, it's still not very friendly. You'll probably want to write a helper tool to pick out the details you're interested in. Or, you can skip the ObjectSpace API altogether and use the next tool in our lineup: the memory_profiler gem.

Using the ObjectSpace API in Ruby 2.1, the memory_profiler gem can collect and report on *a lot* of information about how your program is

making use of memory. Like with the stackprof gem, you have to manually activate memory profiling in your code. With the memory_profiler
gem there's also an additional step. After profiling a block of code the
MemoryProfiler::report method returns a report object you then use
to print out the contents of the report to the terminal:

```
require("memory_profiler")

report = MemoryProfiler.report do
  ...
end
report.pretty_print
```

The report generated by the memory_profiler gem focuses mainly on
two categories of objects: allocated and retained. Allocated objects are
exactly what they sound like...any object created while the block given
to MemoryProfiler::report was running. Retained objects are those
that were not released after the block finished. Some of these retained
objects might be classes and modules that live until Ruby terminates,
and some may be leaked objects that are sticking around due to long-
lived references. Allocated and retained objects are reported by the
source-code files that created them. The following is a significantly
trimmed report from the memory_profiler gem:

```
Total allocated 892553
Total retained 4680

allocated memory by gem
-----------------------------------
2.1.1/lib x 75201418
rubygems x 1181583
other x 120

allocated memory by location
-----------------------------------
lib/ruby/2.1.0/net/protocol.rb:153 x 35241433
lib/ruby/2.1.0/csv.rb:1806 x 16217960
lib/ruby/2.1.0/csv.rb:1833 x 16217960
lib/ruby/2.1.0/csv.rb:1783 x 2918998

retained memory by location
-----------------------------------
lib/ruby/2.1.0/rubygems/core_ext/kernel_require.rb:55 x 116966
lib/ruby/2.1.0/uri/common.rb:853 x 20440
lib/ruby/2.1.0/x86_64-linux/socket.so:0 x 17676
lib/ruby/2.1.0/uri/common.rb:863 x 11680
```

We've covered a lot of profiling reports and tools in this item. Clearly, if you're trying to track down a performance problem in your Ruby code you have several options to choose from. The tools you choose largely depend on which version of Ruby you're working with. For versions before Ruby 2.1, the ruby-prof gem is your best option. But starting with Ruby 2.1 ruby-prof can be complemented with the stackprof and memory_profiler gems. With these additions to your toolbox you'll be surprised at how easy it can be to improve the performance of your Ruby programs.

Things to Remember

+ Use a profiling tool to collect evidence before you start modifying poorly performing code.

+ Prefer the ruby-prof gem to the standard profile library. The former is much faster and produces several different reports.

+ If you're using Ruby 2.1 or later you should consider using the stackprof and memory_profiler gems.

Item 47: Avoid Object Literals in Loops

Quick, how many objects does this code create?

```
errors.any? {|e| %w(F1 F2 F3).include?(e.code)}
```

This is fairly idiomatic code, something you're likely to see out in the wild. If the errors array has *n* elements this code will create up to *4n* objects. The reason there's a range of possibilities is due to the any? method from the Enumerable module. It invokes its block once for each element in the array as long as the block returns false. Once the block returns true, the any? method can short-circuit and avoid iterating over the remaining elements. That explains the potential number of iterations, but where does the 4 come in? Recall that the %w notation used in the block is equivalent to—but more efficient than—using split:

```
"F1 F2 F3".split
```

In this case, the %w notation creates an array containing three strings, and it does this each time the block is called. As soon as the include? method completes, the newly created array becomes unreachable garbage, which Ruby will eventually sweep away. Just in case you think this has something to do with %w, here's the same code with an array literal instead:

```
errors.any? {|e| ["F1", "F2", "F3"].include?(e.code)}
```

Both versions create four objects each time the block is invoked. The problem is obviously that the array of strings should be a constant. It's never mutated or assigned to a variable, which might be part of the reason Ruby programmers tend to overlook these unnecessary allocations. But it's not just the allocations themselves that are problematic. Each time an object is created in Ruby it might trigger a partial or full garbage-collection run. This simple looking line of code could turn out to be a performance bottleneck. (But remember to avoid jumping to conclusions about performance problems and follow the advice in Item 46.)

The other part of the problem is that we don't write explicit loops in Ruby. The closest you can get is by using the for keyword, but that's rarely used in practice. Instead, Ruby programmers prefer the iterator pattern and supply blocks to methods like any? and each, which may then invoke these blocks any number of times. So, creating these temporary objects in hidden loops is the real problem. Thankfully, the fix is easy. Promote object literals in loops (which are disguised as blocks) to constants if the objects are never mutated:

```ruby
FATAL_CODES = %w(F1 F2 F3).map(&:freeze).freeze
```

```ruby
def fatal? (errors)
  errors.any? {|e| FATAL_CODES.include?(e.code)}
end
```

This version moves the array literal out of the loop and into a constant. Following the advice in Item 4, the constant is also frozen so that it can't be accidentally mutated. With this change the four objects will be created once when the code is loaded, instead of each time through the loop. As a result, the number of allocations is reduced along with the risk of invoking the garbage collector. I recommend you do this with any object literal. But before you go and start refactoring, let's look at one surprising change to Ruby starting in version 2.1. Consider this variation of the loop we've been reviewing:

```ruby
errors.any? {|e| e.code == "FATAL"}
```

This code has the same problem as the others, albeit on a smaller scale. Each time the block is invoked it will create a string that is used solely for comparison and then quickly becomes garbage. If you're using a version of Ruby prior to 2.1 the fix is the same as above—promote this string literal to a constant. But if you're using 2.1 or later you have another option:

```ruby
errors.any? {|e| e.code == "FATAL".freeze}
```

Frozen string literals in Ruby 2.1 and later are equivalent to constants. The block in the previous example will only allocate a single string on its first invocation. All subsequent invocations will use the same string object. As a matter of fact, once a frozen string literal is introduced it can be shared throughout the entire program. So, if the string used in this block had been allocated previously the block wouldn't allocate any new objects. Essentially, these strings act like symbols with the added benefit that they can be garbage collected when they're no longer being used. Just remember: This optimization only works if you freeze a string *literal*. It doesn't have the same effect if you freeze an arbitrary string object.

Things to Remember

+ Promote object literals in loops (which are disguised as blocks) to constants if the objects are never mutated.

+ Frozen string literals in Ruby 2.1 and later are equivalent to constants and are shared throughout the running program.

Item 48: Consider Memoizing Expensive Computations

A very common optimization pattern used in Ruby that you should be familiar with is memoization. You've probably written code using this pattern without realizing it. Consider this snippet of code, which can be found in nearly every web application in one form or another:

```ruby
def current_user
  @current_user ||= User.find(logged_in_user_id)
end
```

Thanks to the "||=" operator, the User::find method is only invoked once and its result is memoized in the @current_user variable. There's a lot going on in this single line of code so let's take a closer look by expanding the "||=" operator:

```ruby
@current_user || @current_user = User.find(logged_in_user_id)
```

Now it should be clear that if @current_user is false or nil then User::find will be called. In that case, the result from User::find will be stored in @current_user. On the other hand, if @current_user already has a value that Ruby considers true then its value will be returned instead of evaluating the right-hand side of the "||" operator. As long as the @current_user instance variable has a non-false, non-nil value then the current_user method will return that value instead of calling User::find.

This, of course, is a caching technique. Suppose for a moment that this method belongs to a request object for a web application. Many layers throughout the application need to query the request object to discover various details about the current user. If it weren't for the memoization, each call to `current_user` would trigger a call to `User::find`, which presumably queries a database. Caching the result of an expensive method call like this can have a major impact on performance. Let's look at another example. Consider this:

```ruby
def shipped? (order_id)
  file = fetch_confirmation_file

  if file
    status = parse_confirmation_file(file)
    status[order_id] == :shipped
  end
end
```

The `shipped?` method takes an order ID and checks to see if that order has shipped from the warehouse. To do that it has to pull the latest confirmation file from the warehouse and look into the file for an order's status. The obvious problem with this method is that it fetches and parses the confirmation file each time it's called. One possible way to improve this would be to factor the fetching and parsing out of the `shipped?` method and place it into the `initialize` method. Another valid solution is to use memoization:

```ruby
def shipped? (order_id)
  @status ||= begin
    file = fetch_confirmation_file
    file ? parse_confirmation_file(file) : {}
  end
  @status[order_id] == :shipped
end
```

In this version, the `@status` variable holds a hash that contains the status of all orders from the warehouse's confirmation file. If this variable hasn't yet been initialized then the right-hand side of the "`||=`" operator will be evaluated, which happens to be a `begin` block. As you know, nearly everything in Ruby is an expression, and a `begin` block is no different. Evaluating a `begin` block will return the value from its last expression. So, in this example, the `@status` variable will be set to either the return value from `parse_confirmation_file` or an empty hash. After the `@status` variable is assigned a hash from the `begin` block it won't evaluate that block again. This means you can call the `shipped?` method as many times as you'd like and it will only fetch and parse the confirmation file once.

As you can see, adding memoization to your code is rather simple. You know what that means right? There's probably a catch. Let's turn our attention to some of the subtle problems that crop up when using memoization.

First, how long do you suppose you should cache the result of a method? With the `current_user` example, the memoization was self-resetting with each web request. Other uses of memoization might last quite a bit longer, maybe even for the duration of a running program. You should consider how long a method should be memoized and whether you need to provide a method that resets the memoization by setting the caching variable to `nil`.

In more complex situations, the method you want to memoize might have arguments that need to be taken into account. Consider the `lookup` method, which builds a cache based on an argument:

```ruby
def lookup (key)
  @cache ||= {} # Make sure @cache exists.

  @cache[key] ||= begin
    ...
  end
end
```

The `lookup` method is memoized with a dependency on its argument. It will only perform the expensive computation (the `begin` block) once for each possible key value. That is, if you call the `lookup` method more than once with the same key it will only evaluate the `begin` block a single time. If you call it with a key that hasn't yet been cached then the `begin` block will be evaluated. Adding additional arguments into the mix increases the complexity. For each additional argument you need to decide if the cache depends on it and if so how to construct a hash key that includes all of the dependencies.

Another potential problem to consider is whether the method you want to memoize has side effects that can't be skipped. At the beginning of this item we looked at the `current_user` method. It clearly has a side effect in that it queries a database. This just happens to be a side effect we want to only happen once per request. But what if a method has other side effects such as mutating instance variables or writing to a log file? Memoizing methods like that might improve the performance for part of the code but completely break the logic in another. Always make sure you consider the consequences of skipped side effects due to memoization.

Take a moment to look back at the `shipped?` method and notice that it always returns `true` or `false`. This is much safer than methods like current_user, which return mutable objects. Consider what happens when the User object returned from current_user is modified by a caller. Since current_user always returns the same variable, every call after the mutation will be exposed to those changes. When this isn't desirable you should consider returning frozen objects from memoized methods.

Finally, the biggest question you should ask yourself before employing memoization is whether it's actually necessary. Follow the advice in Item 46 and profile your program before you jump to conclusions about its performance. Adding memoization to a method might be easy, but as we've seen, it comes with some risks. Make sure you actually need it before you start sprinkling it throughout your code.

Things to Remember

+ Consider providing a method that sets the caching variable to nil as a way to reset the memoization.

+ Make sure you consider the consequences of skipped side effects due to memoization.

+ If you don't want callers to be able to modify a caching variable you should consider returning frozen objects from memoized methods.

+ Profile your code to see if you need memoization before you start using it.

Epilogue

The ideas presented in this book stretch much further than the space between its covers. Thanks to the many contributors in the community, Ruby is a living, breathing project that continues to evolve. I encourage you to get involved, whether it's through working on Ruby itself or by releasing your hard work as a RubyGem. Give back to the community that has so graciously given to you. At the same time, demand that we all work harder to create reliable, secure software that pushes the boundaries of what is possible.

Our journey through this book and its topics has been fun for me, and hopefully enjoyable for you, too. My hope is that, in some way, I have helped you and thus impacted the software you work on. I appreciate any feedback you might have for me as well as any questions that remain unanswered. You can reach me through the website for this book at http://effectiveruby.com. Thank you for reading!

Index

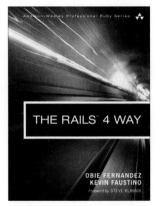
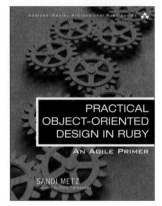
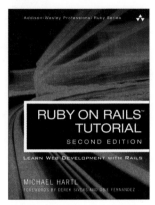
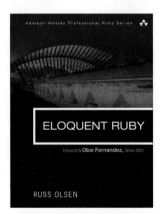